BE IN THE ROOM

LAUREN MORRISON

Honey Blossom Press
www.honeyblossompress.com
@honeyblossompress

ISBNs: 9781967565160 (trade paperback),
9781967565177 (ebook)

Printed in the United States of America

HONEY BLOSSOM PRESS

BE IN THE THE ROOM

CONTENTS

INTRODUCTION
Welcome to My Room

Dammit WELCOME to my room!

And yes, the moment I wrote that, *of course* my brain cued up that nineties R&B classic by Silk: *"There's a meeting in my bedrooooommmm"*

Go ahead. Fan yourself and wipe the sweat off your brow. I'll wait.

But don't get *too* excited—that's not the kind of room I'm talking about.

I'm talking about *this* room. The one I built for *you* to be authentic, vulnerable, and emotionally safe. Not so that you can be coddled and held, but so that you can be challenged and stretched in scary, but rewarding ways. A space where it's not just okay—but necessary—to be everything you were told not to be in order to succeed. This is your permission slip to be raw. Emotional. Messy. Unrehearsed. Raw. Unpolished. This is the room where high achieving doesn't require high performing twenty-four seven.

This is the room where "put together" is optional, and truth is the dress code. Why? Because that's what it took for me to write this damn book with my whole-ass face on the cover.

Which, by the way, do you think I *wanted* my face on this cover? Absolutely not! Just the *idea* of putting my face on a book cover made me want to hurl. It felt loud. Audacious. *Too much.* Like one giant *"Who the hell does she think she is?"*

But here's the thing: That voice? That feeling? It's nothing new. That voice followed me everywhere from the stage to the boardroom.

I heard it when I auditioned to be a Beyoncé impersonator in a Destiny's Child tribute band at eighteen. (Spoiler: I booked it. If you want to learn how to lead, pretend to be Beyoncé for three years. It changed everything.)

I heard it when I was offered an executive role in corporate at thirty years old. When I left a six-figure salary and stable life in Canada to bet on myself—and my purpose—in Los Angeles. When I built my coaching practice from scratch. And yep, I heard it again every time I sat down to write this book.

Those thoughts brought on a sour taste in the back of my throat. I used to read them as signs that I was reaching too high and needed to humble myself. That the only reason they are present is because they are warranted.

Reality? They were signs that I'm itching and **deserving** of something bigger.

But what about you?

Maybe you think you know what success looks like. Hell, by most standards, you probably already are successful. Climbed the corporate ladder or built a start-up from scratch? You already get it.

But I'm going to bet there's a fire in you—a burning, insatiable hunger that refuses to be satisfied by any achievement. That voice in your head? The one that says, *"This isn't enough, there's more to this game"*? That's why you're here.

If you've picked up this book, I already know you're a special breed of person. You're accomplished, likely a professional or entrepreneur who has blown past not just society's expectations but perhaps even your own. You've amassed achievements that used to be the stuff of your wildest dreams.

You're also ambitious, no stranger to taking calculated risks—some that have propelled you into new heights, and others that were, well, formative experiences to say the least.

Your life, both personal and professional, is a highlight reel of success that gets applause from almost everyone around you. But what this well-curated spectacle doesn't show your band of supporters, family, colleagues, and friends is the more complex inner narrative.

They don't see the internal tension between your hunger for more—more impact, more passion, more life—and the guilt you sometimes bear for wanting it. They can't see the loneliness. The isolation that trails your success. They can't feel your frustration that despite all you've achieved, there's a level of greatness you can't seem to grasp.

If you are nodding your head, then read on, because I wrote this book for you.

That hunger? It's not greed. It's not ego.

It's *knowing*.

Knowing there's a version of you—more alive, more powerful, more *you*—waiting to be unleashed. It's knowing you weren't meant to simply earn your seat at the table. You were meant to shift the whole damn room.

And yet...

You shrink. You second-guess. You doubt your instincts in rooms where power is present but safety isn't. You deliver brilliance in one meeting and spiral for days replaying what you didn't say in another, all while carrying wins that no longer light you up and dreams too terrifying to say out loud.

Sound familiar?

Then this book is your mirror. Your match to reignite that spark. Your beautiful release, like that first glass of wine at six p.m. on a Friday night (or whatever you use to come down after a long week).

And no, we aren't going to do this with positive affirmations and sanitized advice about "stepping into your power" or "claiming your inner king/queen" (yeah, I saw you roll your eyes just now). That fluffy, pandering stuff may work for some, but not you. You're too smart for that—and frankly, too tired.

Instead, I'll show you the invisible narratives that keep brilliant people like you stuck in rooms that no longer fit. We'll unpack the systems that reward performance but punish authenticity.

And we'll rewrite the rules—on your terms.

No more contorting. No more contending. It's time to own the room like you built it. Just like my client Jonelle did.

Let me show you what that looks like in real life.

Jonelle's Story—From Shrinking to Sovereign

By all external accounts, Jonelle was winning.

She had the title, the trust, the double-booked calendar, and the reputation for getting things done.

But behind the power suit and the perfectly curated LinkedIn profile? Jonelle was tired. Not just "I need a nap" tired, but soul tired. From constantly questioning herself. From shrinking just enough to avoid being labeled "too much." From swallowing her brilliance in rooms that didn't feel safe to speak in.

Her mind was loud with the usual suspects: *Am I doing enough? Am I enough? Will I be seen as competent, or combative?*

Through our work together, we peeled back belief systems that told her she had to choose between being powerful and being palatable.

We rewired them, slowly but surely. She built new strategies, new language, a new internal compass. And with each step forward, she became a version of herself that would've felt unrecognizable just months before. And right on cue, life said, "Let's see what you've got."

In the wake of a new U.S. president elect, Jonelle's organization was rocked. Her leader let go. The projects that had once made her excited to get out of bed? Shut down or deprioritized. And just like that, Jonelle found herself dropped into a department she'd never worked in, leading a team she didn't know, navigating a high-stakes, politically charged project that had completely stalled out.

No playbook or hand-holding.

Just her. And the voice that had once whispered, *"You're not ready,"* suddenly had a megaphone.

Now, an earlier version of her might've played it safe. Played small. Nodded in meetings, smiled politely, and emailed suggestions "for consideration."

But not this time.

Jonelle didn't shrink. She stepped in.

She facilitated heated conversations, asked the questions no one else had the guts to ask, and spotted miscommunication and misalignment others were too siloed to see. Instead of dominating the room, she disarmed it.

As she told me afterward: *"It felt good to stand on what I know I bring to the table without being scared to bring it forward or speak up. Without being scared to question high-level leadership on how they were doing things and to do it all in a way that felt like me. That's when it clicked."*

The result? That project moved fast. And it didn't just succeed; it helped save forty million dollars in funding that would've been lost to families who needed it most.

But the real win wasn't the money. It was this: *"I made it bigger than them. I made it bigger than me. That's why it felt powerful."*

And this book? It's about *that* power.

The power you already *have* but might still be afraid to trust. The kind of power that doesn't wait for permission. The kind that doesn't ask, *"Will they like me if I speak up?"* The kind that says, *"I'm going to speak anyway."*

This book is for the Jonelle in *you*. The part that's done contorting. Done shrinking. The part that's ready to walk into every room—boardroom, breakroom, or family dinner—as your *whole* self. Because if you haven't noticed?

The rooms are shifting. And they need *you* in them.

Jonelle's Story Isn't a One-Off

For more than a decade, I've built, led, and developed high-performing teams across the public and private sectors. I've managed multimillion-dollar portfolios, navigated executive politics, and mentored leaders across industries.

But more importantly, I've coached hundreds of ambitious professionals. From C-suite executives to entrepreneurs to emerging leaders, I've helped them through massive personal and professional transitions. People who, on paper, had it all figured out but still felt stuck, burned out, or quietly unfulfilled.

Through my coaching frameworks rooted in neuroscience, emotional intelligence, and high-performance psychology, my clients have:

- Landed executive promotions they were once too scared to go for.

- Launched and scaled impact-driven businesses.

- Built unshakable confidence after years of contorting themselves to fit into corporate molds.

- Rewritten their internal narratives from *"Who am I to do this?"* to *"Why the hell not me?"*

I've worked with award-winning executives, start-up founders, diversity, equity, and inclusion (DEI) leaders, artists, nonprofit changemakers, and everything in between. This book isn't based on one person's perspective; it's a synthesis of patterns I've seen emerge across industries, identities, and ambitions.

I've sat in boardrooms with billion-dollar decision-makers and on Zoom calls with burned-out women sobbing between strategy sessions. I've seen both the systems and the souls behind success. And I've made it my mission to bridge the gap between the two.

So no, I'm not some guru selling six-figure templates or manifestation hacks. I'm a coach, strategist, and lived-it-the-hard-way practitioner who knows what it takes to burn the old blueprint and build a career and life that actually *fits*.

And that's exactly what I'm here to help you do.

Why I Wrote This Book

You've done everything "right." You've climbed the ladder, shattered ceilings, earned your seat—yet something still feels *off*.

I've been where you are.

Haunted by the conundrum of having "everything" yet desperate for a purpose that was uniquely my own. I've wrestled with complex emotions, societal expectations, and self-imposed limitations. Through my years of coaching people of all backgrounds, I've found that these feelings are not just personal but universally experienced. People's need for a guide to navigate the murky waters of high-level success was not just evident but urgent.

Because women like Jonelle—and maybe women like you—are done bending to fit in.

You're technically in the room, but you're not fully in it. Not as your whole self. Not with your full voice.

And the truth is, the workplace—hell, the world—isn't making it easier to show up fully.

The System Is Backsliding

I don't subscribe to being overly political; however, we can't ignore some of the facts that have shifted our landscape in the early days of writing this book.

In 2025, President Trump signed Executive Order 14173, banning DEI requirements for federal contractors and striking down key equity initiatives across public institutions; promoting so-called "merit" over inclusion. And yeah, I said "so-called merit" because "merit" is defined by the dominant culture (often white, male, able-bodied, and straight) and pretends that talent and effort alone determines success. But *we* know that access, networks, proximity to power, and systemic privilege often carry more weight than performance alone.

A McKinsey study found that Black and Latina women receive less support from managers, have fewer sponsors, and are less likely to be given high-visibility projects—all of which are crucial to "earning" merit in the eyes of leadership.[1]

But none of this is news to you, so I won't bore you with the statistics. You don't need numbers to validate your experience. You feel it every. Single. Day. But if you're anything like me, you've just learned to accept it as "normal." Never really questioning or challenging, just accepting (more on this acceptance in a future chapter).

But I digress. Back to the infamous "let's cancel DEI" executive order. Overnight, companies that once paraded diversity pledges began rewriting them in invisible ink. Corporate leaders replaced commitment with caution.

According to the *Harvard Business Review*, by mid-2025, over 90% of Fortune 500 companies had either scaled back or removed their DEI strategies, citing legal ambiguity and political pressure.[2]

The impact? Programs once designed to support underrepresented professionals vanished. Advocacy became optics. Safety became survival. And while systems retract, you're still expected to expand. To lead. To speak up.

To shrink less, smile more, and never let them see you sweat.

And the toll is staggering.

---

1   McKinsey & Company, & LeanIn.Org. (2024). *Women in the workplace 2024.* https://www.mckinsey.com/women-in-the-workplace-2024

2   Harvard Business Review. (2025, July–August). *Achieve DEI goals without DEI programs.* Retrieved from /mnt/data/Coaching Enrolment Script.pdf

Burnout is at an all-time high. According to the same McKinsey 2024 Women in the Workplace Report, 43% of women leaders say they are burned out, and the number climbs to 54% for women of color. Many cite exclusion, lack of recognition, and the constant emotional tax of navigating workplace bias as key contributors.

[3]In fact, nearly one in three Black women in leadership said they considered leaving their jobs not because they lacked the skill or ambition, but because they were tired of feeling unseen and undercut in environments that called for excellence but rarely returned equity.

This isn't a lack of resilience. This is the result of being overextended, under-supported, and gaslit by systems that applaud your drive while quietly resisting your presence.

Bottom line: **You are not set up for success.**

I don't say this to diminish hope. I say this because I deeply want you to stop waiting for the workplace to change. It's no longer an option. Burnout is not the badge of honor you think it is and being a high achiever should not require being half expressed.

So I'll say it again: You are not set up for success.

Let that little tear form in the corner of your eye, and then decide: Are you ready to create it, on your terms?

This book is a reclamation of your agency. A refusal to wait for systems to change before you take action. A blueprint for showing up as your whole self in rooms that weren't built for you and rooms you're ready to build yourself.

---

3   McKinsey & Company, & LeanIn.Org. (2024). *Women in the work-place 2024*. https://www.mckinsey.com/women-in-the-workplace-2024

Before You Go Any Further: A Note on Accountability

After I left my corporate job, people would ask me all the time: *"Do you ever miss it?"*

My answer? *Absolutely.*

Which usually left them blinking at me like I'd just said I missed getting root canals. Let me clarify:

I miss being able to **blame people.** Like, *deeply* miss it. Because let's face it, in a big (or even small) corporation, you could always find someone else to point the finger at.

Revenue in the toilet? Blame marketing.

Project delays? Blame IT or the city.

Morale in the gutter? Blame leadership.

No raises this year? Blame the economy.

Blame was the buffet special and the flavors were savory and endless. But once I stepped into entrepreneurship? **No more buffet.** Just one item on the menu: *me.*

Every decision, every delay, every dip in income? My responsibility. Not the algorithm. Not the market. Not my partner, my kids, or Mercury in retrograde. **Me.** There is *always* something else I can do. An action, thought, or mindset that I can pivot.

It's saying, *"Yeah that's happening. So, what will I do about it next?"*

And if that truth makes you uncomfortable, I get it. Blame is cozy. Blame lets you off the hook. Blame says, *"It's not your fault,"* which conveniently means *"You don't have to change."*

That being said, I need to set a very important tone right now.

If you're not ready to take full ownership of your mindset, your choices, and your outcomes—close this book! Seriously. Don't even waste your time, because nothing in here will work unless you do.

Pauses and then looks around the room

Are they gone? Is it just us now?

Okay, good, because if you're still here it tells me something about who you are. It tells me you're done with waiting. Done with podcast episodes that inspire but never move the needle. Done with outsourcing your power and so unbelievably ready to make moves that actually change things.

This book is for you if:

- You're tired of white-knuckling your way through a life that *looks* good but feels off.
- You've outgrown the version of success you once chased and now you want *more*—not just money, but **meaning**.
- You know you're capable of more, but your own mental roadblocks keep pulling the emergency brake.

Let's be clear: This book isn't some "How to Manifest a Million Dollars in 90 Days" scheme. There are enough Instagram ads for that targeting the person who is feeling so far behind that they are in a rush.

This is about **doing the real work**—the uncomfortable, transformative, no-one-is-coming-to-save-you work—of aligning your ambition with your values so you can build a career, a business, a *life* that actually fits.

Because here's the truth: Burnout doesn't just come from working hard.

It comes from working hard on the *wrong things* with the *wrong mindset* in the *wrong rooms*.

This book is your tool kit for change:

- To stop performing and start leading.
- To stop seeking permission and start taking up space.
- To stop chasing validation and start building on your *value*.

Sounds great, right?

But How Is This Book Going to Help You Do That?

This book is a compass to help you navigate the ups and downs of high achievement. It's not just about theories and research (though you'll find plenty of those because I'm not just making this stuff up to fill the pages); it's also packed with real client stories (names changed, of course) and raw, unfiltered moments from my personal blogs. I'm sharing some of my most vulnerable experiences on the path to success and fulfillment, so you're not just reading about the journey, you're right there with me.

What you're about to read isn't linear—it's transformational. And like all transformation, it will require truth telling, shedding, and rebuilding.

Each phase corresponds with a core part of the book:

Part One: "Giiirrrl, You Put on Weight!"

The Emotional and Invisible Weight of Being "The Strong One"

(Apologies for the potentially triggering title. A bit of a nod to my Caribbean heritage and aunties—if you get it, you get it.)

You've been carrying too much for too long. And no, we're not just talking about your calendar or key performance indicators (KPIs). This is the weight of unspoken expectations, emotional labor, unprocessed resentment, and the need to prove yourself over and over again. You didn't ask for it, but here you are. Let's name it, unpack it, and finally set some of it down.

Part Two: Who Wrote This Script?

Unlearning the Stories That Told You to Shrink

You didn't just wake up with these beliefs about leadership, success, and self-worth. They were shaped by systems, culture, family, and survival. In this stage, we crack them open. We interrogate them. Ditching the ones that no longer serve you, and writing new ones that give you back your "don't fuck with me" edge (by the way, is it too late to include an explicit language warning? Well, it's here now and I can already hear my mom's voice: *"You sound like a common fish woman!"* Sorry, Mom. In the spirit of authenticity, I'm going to say things the way I actually say them).

Part Three: That Thing You Keep Calling Crazy? It's Actually Clarity Claiming The Vision

Now that the old scripts are being rewritten, we get to dream differently. Bigger. Bolder. This is where you begin to see new possibilities: new rooms to enter, new tables to flip, and maybe even new spaces to build from scratch. Not based on what you think others want—but on how you want to feel, lead, and live.

Part Four: You Said You Wanted The Room. Now Stay In It Facing the Hard of Change Head-On

This is where most people stop. Because once you start showing up differently, the room responds—and not always with applause. Boundaries are tested. Systems push back. People get uncomfortable. But this is the fire that forges something unshakable. Your clarity sharpens. Your courage compounds. You stop contorting, and you start commanding.

Part Five: Say It With Your Chest
Be In the Room

This is where you stop asking for permission and start owning your space. Not as a performance, but as practice. You don't need to dim. You don't need to explain. You're not waiting for the room to shift. You *are* the shift.

This isn't just a book. It's a call. To stop surviving success. To stop outsourcing your authority. To step into a version of yourself that feels fully, wildly, unapologetically alive.

Note on Neuroscience in This Book

(Don't you dare yawn! This is the best part.)

In coaching, you'll come across loads of philosophies, ranging from religious and spiritual approaches to wellness focused and beyond. My approach to high-performance coaching is grounded in neuroscience (in other words, how your brain works).

My goal isn't to turn you into a scientist, but to hand you the keys to reclaiming your agency. When you know how your nervous system works, you stop thinking you're broken—and start realizing you're wired for survival in a system that demands suppression.

I want to shed light on something important—the reactions, emotions, and challenges you face, the ones that might trigger shame, guilt, or self-doubt, aren't character flaws. They're actually the result of millions of years of brain evolution, hardwired into us for survival. What helped our ancestors navigate their world doesn't always serve us in today's fast-paced, modern life.

In my work coaching hundreds of clients, I've seen firsthand how understanding this is a game changer. When people realize their struggles are rooted in biology—not personal failure—they shift from feeling defeated to feeling empowered. It's not about blaming yourself; it's about recognizing these instincts for what they are and learning how to work with them instead of against them.

Here are a few key players we'll reference often:

- **Amygdala:** Your fear center. It's designed to protect you but often overreacts to perceived threats (like feedback or failure).

- **Prefrontal cortex:** Your rational mind. This is where self-trust, decision-making, and long-term thinking live.

- **Limbic system:** Your emotional processing hub. It shapes how you attach meaning to experience—and how you respond to stress.

There's a lot deeper and more scientific I can go, but let's be honest, you didn't pick up this book because you want to deeply understand the inner workings of a "hippocampus."

I'm certainly not saying that at the end of this book, you'll be equipped to earn your PhD in neuroscience (unless you already have it, which in that case, *touché*, my friend), but you will understand how to lead with your whole brain—so you can move from reactive to resilient.

Sticky Notes: The Ultimate $3 Brain Hack

If you've been in my world for more than five minutes, you already know: I swear by sticky notes. I use them to plan big moves, map out client strategies, and most of all—I use them to rewire my brain. Every time I identify a new mindset I need to adopt or a behavior I want to shift, I distill it down into a single phrase, write it on a sticky note, and slap it somewhere I can't ignore.

Not in a journal (too easy to stash away).

Not in a digital folder (out of sight, out of mind).

But on my laptop. On the bathroom mirror. On the fridge. Anywhere I'm likely to face resistance or fall back into an old pattern. Because in those moments, I don't need a pep talk. I need a visible, in-my-face reminder that says:

This is how we show up now.

That's why at the top of each chapter in this book, you'll find a sticky note. A bold, unmissable mantra that captures the chapter's essence. If a particular note hits hard or feels like something you need to hear on repeat—**copy it**. Write it down, stick it somewhere meaningful, and let it interrupt your old thinking until your new thinking becomes second nature.

It takes practice, but one day that day will come when you look at that note and realize, *"I don't need this anymore."*

And when that day comes...*ugh!* Trust me, nothing feels better than retiring a sticky note.

Put It into Practice

As a coach, I ask a lot of questions. And the way I've structured this book is no different.

A true coaching mindset means I recognize that YOU are the expert of your own life. My job isn't to tell you what to do—it's to create the space, provide the tools, and ask the right questions so that you can start hearing your own voice more clearly and decide for yourself what you *want* to do.

These sections are designed to help you pause, reflect, and apply what you're reading to your own journey. I'll share expertise, research, personal stories, and client experiences—but none of that will create lasting change unless you take the time to connect it to your own life.

So, here's my challenge to you: Don't just read and nod along. Stop. Reflect. And write it down. Grab a journal, a notepad, or use the space I've created for you within this book—whatever works. Writing isn't just about keeping track of ideas; it's a tool for clarity. It takes the swirl of thoughts in your head and makes them visible, tangible, and actionable.

The books that changed my life and business were the ones that made me stop and do the work—not just consume the ideas but engage with them. That's my hope for you here. Don't just breeze through the pages. Use these moments to listen to yourself, challenge your assumptions, and start building the room you want to be in.

Receipts

I'm not big on positive self-talk or false progress, unless of course these things are grounded in evidence. Proof that you did the thing. That's why at the end of each chapter I've included a section called **Receipts.** This section goes beyond summarizing and serves as proof of transformation.

This section captures what you've learned, unlearned, and actually *done* so you can pause and witness the shift already taking shape. Because if you're doing this book right, you're not just reading. You're *moving*—through mindset blocks, outdated beliefs, and tired narratives that no longer fit where you're headed.

Receipts is your progress report. It documents the internal wins no one else may see but you'll *feel*—the ones that matter most.

It's your moment to say:
- I named something I hadn't said out loud before.
- I questioned a belief that's been running the show for years.
- I made a choice that felt different. Bigger. More aligned.

Growth isn't always loud, but it should be **trackable**. And when your inner critic pipes up and says, *"You're not doing enough,"* you'll have something to point to and say, *"Actually, here's what I've already done."*

Not because you need gold stars, but because you need reminders that you're already becoming who you've been trying to be. It's the checkpoint that proves: *You're not just turning pages. You're turning a corner.*

So, take the time to look back before you leap forward. Because what's coming next? It's going to ask even more of you—and you'll be ready.

My Hope Strategy for You (Because "Hope" is not a Strategy)

By the end of this book, you'll not only understand the intertwining of your own desires and ambitions but will be armed with practical tools for long-term success. You'll leave with a reinvigorated sense of purpose, less guilt, and strategies to endure the challenges that come alongside the journey to lifelong fulfillment.

I ~~hope to~~ **will** ensure that by the final page, you no longer feel the need to explain your excellence or justify your ambition.

I ~~hope to~~ **will** provide you with strategies to stop asking for permission to be powerful.

I ~~hope to~~ **will** empower you stop shrinking to stay safe.

You are not too much. You are not too late. You are not alone.

You are in the room.

Welcome.

Now, let's begin.

Part One
"Giiirrrl, You Put on Weight!"

THE EMOTIONAL (AND INVISIBLE) WEIGHT OF BEING "THE STRONG ONE"

Starve Terry.
Feed Urkel!

#BeInTheRoom

(This will make sense later... promise)

Chapter One

Who Put This Damn Rope Here?
(And Why Did I Let it Stay so Long?)

I remember the moment I felt the rope pull.

I walked into a boardroom full of real estate executives, and even though I was the one invited to lead, all I wanted to do was retreat back to safety. Back to the confines of the space where I didn't question myself. Where I didn't believe that everyone in the room was questioning me.

The rope wasn't visible. But it was real.

An Elephant Never Forgets

Let me tell you a story.

When elephants are young, trainers tie a rope around their ankle and secure it to a stake in the ground. Naturally, what do you think the baby elephant does? It pulls. It tugs. It fights against that rope with all its might. But no matter how hard it tries, it can't break free.

Over time, that baby elephant learns something: there's no point in pulling anymore. Its efforts feel hopeless. So, it stops trying.

And here's the heartbreaking part: that same elephant grows into a powerful adult—thousands of pounds heavier, strong enough to uproot trees. But it no longer needs the stake to stay in place. A rope loosely tied around its ankle is enough to keep it still. Because in its mind, the rope is still stronger than it is.

That's how limiting beliefs work.

We, too, are trained by experiences, by feedback, by moments of pain and rejection that tie ropes around our ankles. And over time, we forget to tug. We stop testing the boundaries that no longer exist.

Especially as women of color, we carry these ropes—the stories we've lived by for so long that we don't realize our conditions, our experiences, our accomplishments have changed. We've grown. We've overcome. We've survived and excelled despite our circumstances. But we keep our eyes fixated on that rope. So our brain leans on old scripts to keep us safe:

- *"Don't speak up."*
- *"Don't stand out."*
- *"Don't risk it."*

But those scripts? Those are the invisible ropes. The ones that introduce self-doubt while negating our growth, achievements, and elephant-like strength.

Like back in that boardroom, for instance.

———— • • ————

As I followed my co-facilitator into the room full of real estate executives, I exhaled a slow and shaky breath.

Logically, I knew I was good enough to be here. I belonged in this room. What evidence did I have? I was invited to speak. To lead.

And yet the eyes of the predominantly white male audience weighed heavy on me, and my shoulders slumped under their gaze. My brain told me it was scrutiny, but I tried to counter the assumption; it could have just as easily been curiosity, maybe even boredom.

So why did I want to curl into myself? Where did this overwhelming urge to walk out come from?

Every fiber of my being told me the executives didn't think I was qualified. The slight grimaces on their lips and their narrowed eyes spoke volumes. Or was it just age?

I'd been in this position before. I knew the drill: *Big smiles, be friendly, but not too friendly.* I didn't want to feed into any hidden desires they may have about "exotic-looking" women. I needed to be assertive, but not too aggressive. I didn't want to reinforce the reason why they didn't let too many "like me" in the rooms to begin with. I wasn't just here for me. Screw this up, and I'd be the reason why other people of color didn't get a chance.

My only choice was to nail the presentation, and they might start to rethink their biases and assumptions about that woman of color back at the office who kept getting overlooked for promotions.

But was that really what these people before me were thinking? Or was it something I was projecting based on very real statistics and stories of others?

Glen began with introductions, just as we'd rehearsed. I stiffened my spine and forced my shoulders away from my ears. Even if it was true that these men thought I wasn't qualified, once they heard my bio, they'd know.

On paper, I looked so damn good. Executive titles. Leader of large teams. Multiple awards won. Exceptional performance ratings. Chosen to deliver multibillion-dollar projects. My bio proved credibility and justified my place in the room. Sure, I might be having a slight crisis of confidence now, and maybe I had to show up twice as good and work twice as hard to make up for the perceived deficit cast upon me by just walking into the room, but my bio was solid.

These men would have no choice but to respect me—

Glen's voice broke through my thoughts. "And this is Lauren. We are going to do things a little differently today." My head snapped to look at him directly. "We aren't going to spend time on our bios—"

Blood rushed to my head, and nothing else he said registered in my brain. This wasn't what we rehearsed.

This was way off-script.

What did he mean we weren't sharing our bios?

My bio was my lifeline. How could these people I was about to guide through leadership exercises know my competence and how deserving I was of their time and attention without proof that I had experience?

Without it, wouldn't they see me as just another pitied diversity hire?

I knew they automatically assumed Glen, a white man, was *meant* to be in the room. His credibility was assumed on sight but they wouldn't give me the sliver of respect I deserved.

Or...maybe I never deserved their respect in the first place.

I wrung my hands, and my gaze darted to the door.

I wanted to run out of the room and never look back. Me being asked to lead this room was a mistake, and I didn't want to give them the chance to prove me right.

I hate that rope. That flimsy rope that my brain swears is impenetrable steel the moment I walk into a room and a quick scan tells me, *"I'm not good enough to be in here."* But more than that, I hate how often I believed it.

Self-Doubt Is Survival When You're "The Only"

I'll never forget debriefing with a colleague, a white male, after a big executive meeting. I said, *"Hey, did you notice that in a room of thirty leaders, there were only two women, including me?"*

He shrugged. *"I don't really look at the room for those things."*

And immediately, I felt like I'd said too much. Embarrassed, I wanted to take the words back with a casual *"Oh yeah, pfffft. Me neither."*

But the truth? I'd been scanning rooms like that for as long as I can remember. I just didn't know it had a name.

It took me years to realize that instinct to clock gender, race, posture, and tone wasn't insecurity. It was survival.

Let me explain.

Imagine you're a zebra on the plains of Tanzania. You step into a clearing and spot a pack of lions. And you're the only zebra around.

You freeze. Your body says run. You don't need to overthink it—you just know you're dinner.

Now picture the same scene, but this time there's a whole herd of zebras. A wall of black and white. You relax just a little. There's safety in numbers. You don't have to bolt. Not yet.

That's what it's like walking into a room where you're "the only." Woman. Person of color. Youngest. Queer. First-gen. Whatever "other" means for you.

Your brain scans for danger, not to be dramatic, but to keep you alive. The problem is, it doesn't know the difference between actual life-or-death danger and the emotional risk of judgment, rejection, or exclusion.

Your brain doesn't care if it's a lion or a LinkedIn message left on *Read*. A threat is a threat. The name of the threat your brain is trying to protect you from: embarrassment.

Sounds petty, but stay with me.

Embarrassment—being seen and possibly judged—used to mean exile from the group. No group means no food, no fire, no safety. So, your brain learned to play it safe. To blend in. To shut up. To scan the room, stick to the script, and survive.

That script? It's been programmed by culture, experience, trauma, and systems that were never designed with you in mind.

Now mix that ancient survival wiring with a modern opportunity, like going after a promotion, launching a business, or leaving a job that's sucking your soul dry, and guess what happens?

The panic sets in.

Not because you're weak. Not because you're unqualified. But because you're about to step out into a field of proverbial lions and mess with your default future.

Your default future is the version of your life that plays out if you change absolutely nothing. It's predictable, it's familiar, and your brain loves it. So, the minute you entertain the idea of something bigger—something different—your brain throws a tantrum.

Who do you think you are?

You're not ready.

They'll laugh at you.

You're going to mess this up.

Quite literally anything it can think of to keep you in the safety and cover of the bushes. These aren't divine signs from the universe. They're just outdated defense mechanisms, just like those imaginary ropes.

So what do you do?

You start by noticing the rope. Notice the belief. The lie. The script that's looping in your head. Then? Tug on it.

Disrupt the autopilot. Ask: Is this thought useful? Is it even true?

If your default belief is, *"I don't belong in this room. They're going to see right through me,"* you don't need to flip to Beyoncé-level confidence in one shot.

Start small:

"I was invited to this room. That means something."

"I've done hard things before. I can do this too."

"I'm not here to impress them. I'm here to add value."

That's how you start flexing the muscle of belief. Slowly. Repeatedly. Especially when it's uncomfortable.

And then? You wait.

That's the part no one tells you. It takes time for your body to catch up to the truth your brain is learning to believe. Those first ten seconds in a scary room feel like a eternity. But if you stay, something shifts.

You take a deep breath, speak, and realize you're not just surviving, you're leading. You're untying the rope.

Untying the Rope... No, Wait, I Mean Feeding Urkel

Wait, what?

At this point, you might be thinking: *Damn, Lauren, I'm still trying to process elephants, ropes, zebras, lions, and ancient survival mechanisms. You're gonna throw a nineties sitcom character in the mix?*

I sure am!

I know my university English professor is pulling out a red marker somewhere, but she's not here, this is *my* book, and dammit, this Urkel analogy works, so bear with me!

See, here's the sneaky thing about self-doubt. Even once we recognize that it's not truth, it still feels true. Why? Because these limiting beliefs have been living rent-free in your brain for the last decade. Just collecting evidence and data to support why it needs to continue to exist. That you *still* need protection.

Almost like that belief has been doing weighted back squats in your brain for years. Decades, maybe. Which means it's *jacked*. Like, full-on bodybuilder vibes. Big chest. Loud voice. Think Terry Crews at the gym, pounding protein shakes, flexing in the mirror, and getting stronger every time you've made a decision that aligned with it.

Now, that new belief you want to implement? Yeah, it's more Steve Urkel right now (this reference assumes you are familiar with nineties Black sitcoms, but I encourage you to do a quick Google search to get the full effect of this visual). Thin. Underfed. Nerdy little voice like, *"Did I do that?"*

But that's the beauty of neuroplasticity (yes, we're bringing science into this). You can bulk up the new belief, but only if you start feeding it.

And the protein it needs? **Evidence.**

Start collecting it.

Times you did the thing. Times you trusted yourself and it worked. Times you showed up, spoke up, stood tall, made magic.

Every time you act in alignment with that new belief, you feed Urkel and starve Terry. Give it a month, and suddenly it's Terry who?

And Urkel? Well, he's not so skinny anymore. He's standing taller. Speaking louder. Suddenly he's transformed into Stefan Urquelle (look that one up too if you're not familiar) and owns the room.

When you stop fighting your limiting beliefs and start working with them, something shifts. They stop being roadblocks and start becoming launchpads that push you to grow, get creative, and build resilience. Instead of holding you back, they become part of your story—a valuable part— helping you navigate the ups and downs that come with growing, personally and professionally.

So, when the limiting narratives consume your brain and insist you aren't good enough, smart enough, or strong enough to take on the next challenge, remember that these thoughts are simply a human reaction to your desire for change. It's a defense mechanism desperate to keep you in pseudo-safety and away from the potential risks (and greatness) of the future you're dreaming of. Because of this, it's not enough to think you are ready for your goals; you need to be able to take the first step toward them.

Putting It into Practice

Before you begin, think of something you're holding yourself back from right now. It could be an action you know you want to take, a leap you want to make, or a difficult conversation you want to have.

Hold that in your mind as you work through these prompts.

What is the biggest challenge you face in doing this thing?

(Example: "I don't have enough time with everything else going on in my life.")

Your response:

What is the story you are telling yourself that supports this challenge?

(Example: "Everyone else's needs are more of a priority right now.")

Your response:

What do you believe about yourself that supports this story?

(Example: "I'm not important enough to prioritize.")

Your response:

Trace the origin. How long has this belief existed for you?

Think of a time when you first recognized yourself believing it. Is it tied to a past experience, feedback, or something you've internalized over time?

Your response:

What's the rope keeping you from?

How does this belief function like that rope around the elephant's ankle? In what ways might it be keeping you small—even though you've outgrown it?

Your response:

Flip the script.

Write a new, empowering thought to challenge the belief.

(Example: "I belong here. I am equipped and ready.")

Your response:

Evidence Check

List 1–3 pieces of evidence that support your new belief.

(Example: "I was invited to this meeting because of my expertise." "I've succeeded in unfamiliar situations before.")

Your response:

What small step can you take today to test this new belief?

(Example: Speak up in a meeting. Ask for feedback. Raise your hand to take on an assignment outside of your job scope that adds value.)

Your response:

Did that reflection feel heavy?

Good. It's supposed to.

It should sting a little to see, in black and white, a belief that's been running the show behind the scenes, guiding your choices, your confidence, and your direction. You might even feel a bit embarrassed that something so outdated has had *that* much power over you.

But here's the good news: Now that you've seen it, you can't *unsee* it.

You'll hear it when it tries to scream its way back into control. And when it does, you get to respond with something like, *"Hey—nope. We said we're not doing that shit anymore."*

And that's how you change. Not by waiting until the rope disappears, but by realizing you've been strong enough to break it all along.

Receipts

Proof that you showed up and started shifting

You didn't just read about limiting beliefs. You met yours face to face, and tugged on the damn rope. Let's review your receipts from Chapter One, shall we?

You did the hard part

- You named the belief that's been holding you back.

- You traced its roots—not to shame yourself, but to understand your survival strategy.

- You called out the lie for what it is: protection disguised as truth.

- You flipped the script.

- You wrote a new belief—maybe shakily, but it's there.

- You found evidence to support it. Real, lived proof.

- You took a step toward practicing it, even if that step felt small or scary.

You started feeding Urkel

- You recognized how your old belief got Terry Crews jacked by years of unchallenged repetition.

- You committed to strengthening a new narrative. One rooted in your strength, your worth, and your belonging.

- You accepted that you don't need to feel ready. You just need to start collecting evidence.

And most importantly:

You didn't flinch when the truth stung. You stayed. You wrote it down. You gave yourself a new story. That's not small. That's power.

Your Next Move

This week, identify one limiting belief that's been keeping you playing small. Name it. Challenge it. And most importantly—take one small, intentional action that aligns with the belief you want to hold instead.

As you do this, notice what resistance surfaces. Pay close attention to a quiet, familiar voice that may whisper, *"But I already have enough."*

On the surface, it sounds like gratitude. But look deeper. Sometimes that thought isn't about true contentment. It's fear, disguised as satisfaction. It's your brain's way of keeping you safe, urging you not to want too much, not to stretch, not to risk.

But BEING IN THE ROOM means daring to want more. Not out of greed, but out of alignment with who you are becoming. It means claiming your space fully, unapologetically, and expanding into the rooms that are waiting for you.

So, as your next move: redefine "enough" for yourself. Not based on what others expect or what feels safe, but based on what this season of your life is calling you toward. The moment you do, you take another powerful step toward truly being in the room. Not just physically present, but fully seen, fully heard, and fully expressed.

Safe and
fulfilled
are not the
same thing

#BeInTheRoom

Chapter Two

It's Not Enough – How to Redefine What Is

Who needs enemies when your inner voice is ready to criticize and sabotage you twenty-four seven? Even your archnemesis in real life has to take breaks from planning your demise and undermining your dreams.

But your inner voice? That isn't going anywhere. It's sitting, armed and ready to spin tales that convince you that you aren't worthy of something better than what you have right now and that you aren't deserving of good things.

And if, by some miracle, positive and hopeful thoughts slip through the cracks to begin to persuade you that perhaps you do deserve better, there's another voice ready to remind you that you should simply be grateful for what you have. It'll tell you a story centered on something like, *"Maybe you are worthy of more, but you shouldn't want more. Because 'more' is for greedy assholes."*

And that's exactly the story I subscribed to when I first began to feel unsatisfied in life—a greedy, undeserving asshole.

(What? You don't talk to yourself this way sometimes? Just me? All right, cool, cool.)

I'd recently received a promotion in my fancy tech corporate job and my first reaction was excitement. I remember looking at the offer and thinking, *I get to earn this money? There are so. Many. Zeros.*

It was surreal to be given the opportunity to make so much money and to be recognized as someone deserving of a promotion.

I should be grateful.

So why wasn't I?

Success Without Joy

I officially had the life countless people wish for: the director position, a big house in the suburbs with a pool and a home theater, an adoring husband, and two beautiful and healthy kids. I was a woman of color in the tech industry, of all places, making over six figures and being handed leadership positions and opportunities to grow.

People finally saw me for my worth in the corporate space.

But there was a pit in my stomach. It wasn't quite dread, but something close...dissatisfaction. A hunger for more that I couldn't squash no matter how many promotions I landed. The emptiness at my core was in a constant battle with the voices in my head screaming that I should be grateful.

By all definitions, I was doing well. I was kicking ass and climbing the ranks in my company.

But the kicker was that I didn't even really like my job.

Sure, I was good at it, but it wasn't something I got *excited* about. There were aspects I liked, particularly the role of leading people and solving problems. But I was feeling disconnected. Technology wasn't an industry I was passionate about. I didn't grow up answering the question *"What do you want to be when you grow up?"* with *"An IT operations and strategy leader at one of the country's biggest and fastest-developing tech companies."*

Surprising, I know.

Maybe I didn't know exactly what I wanted to be when I was just a girl, but as I grew up, I knew I wanted to do something that inspired not only me but the people around me.

And if I was being honest, I didn't care a lick about internet circuits or rolling out top technology to businesses across the nation.

I found myself excelling at work but avoiding all conversations about my job after I clocked out. I didn't care to tell people what I did for a living or spruce up my LinkedIn page with posts about my accomplishments.

I realized with each promotion that I didn't want to be associated with my job outside of the office. I was so much more than my corporate job.

Even though I harbored these thoughts and a deep unhappiness for years, I let my inner critic and my limiting beliefs take the reins. I undermined myself and kept my foot on the throat of my dreams and wishes, never letting up even to imagine the possibility of something more.

And while we all have our own limiting beliefs to wrangle, I made sure those around me didn't just have to deal with their limiting inner voice, but also *my* voice, loud and clear. I'm specifically referring to my husband here.

I'd love to tell you that I'm in a relationship where I supported my partner and his desire for more. His desire to do better in life so our family could reap the benefits.

Nope. I seemed to have missed that memo.

I would listen to my husband, Chris, admit he was unhappy with his job or felt stagnant, and I would jump in to remind him to *"be grateful"* and shame him with statements like, *"Why can't you just be happy with what you have?"* As a Black man in corporate, he was very successful and lucky to be in a leadership position.

We both were.

And it was frustrating that neither of us seemed to be able to internalize that fact.

As time went on, and my dissatisfaction only worsened, I realized I had to face the music. I needed to figure out what exactly I was unhappy with. Maybe if I named it, I could be better at shoving it aside and getting back to my perfectly fine life.

I looked around and saw people in my neighborhood and online doing things that I couldn't. Parents would walk their kids to and from school, friends reconnected on weekend cottage trips, and people seemed to enjoy life in a way I wasn't.

I wanted a job I liked, one where it meant something to someone. I wanted to provide impact and purpose.

I wanted autonomy over my time and to be more present in my kids' lives.

But as I got clear about my end goal, why did I feel like shit about wanting this life?

Where did I get the notion that I should be satisfied with what other people gave me? Why was this statement woven into my very soul?

The Black(ish) Elephant in the Room

If you saw my picture on the cover of this book and thought to yourself "what is she?" you definitely wouldn't be the first. On appearance, I'm what you would call racially ambiguous. My parents are Black, white, and Indian, but even they can't agree on what I am.

And any mixed person reading this knows the story of how multiracial children grow up feeling like they don't belong to any side of their ethnicity, and they are constantly outcasts. I actually have a very difficult time talking about my race and my origins because no matter how I identify, someone is always ready to counter me with a statement like, *"Yeah, but you're not really X, though, are you?"* That discomfort doesn't magically disappear, so you can imagine the lingering feelings of unease and unbelonging as I navigated the workplace in adulthood.

When I looked around the meeting rooms, walked the halls of the office, and visited customer sites, I noticed that there was hardly anyone who looked like me. And there were *never* any executives who looked like me.

That lack of representation becomes ingrained in your psyche. No one ever needs to tell you overtly that you won't ever become successful because of your ethnicity, or because of your gender, or your age. Scan enough rooms where decisions are made, power is in abundance, and authority thrives—the narrative writes itself.

When there isn't anyone who looks like you, you believe those positions aren't for you. And this was a belief I felt in the fabric of my being.

But it wasn't just the lack of diversity in my colleagues who added to the belief that I shouldn't be in the room. I didn't see examples of people in my family who were navigating corporate spaces at this level. Family values are another ingredient in forming limiting beliefs.

Growing up, my family was comfortably middle class and a first-generation immigrant family. My dad is a man with strong opinions, and he made his known whenever he had the floor. And his strongest one: *"Rich people are unhappy pricks."*

Yes, you read that right: Rich people are unhappy pricks.

In my family, money was considered the source of all family dysfunction and a symbol of misery.

The typical immigrant parent narrative is that they move to a new country for a better life and opportunities for their children. With the caveat that the children live in a standardized script of success and don't take risks to unravel all the parents sacrificed.

Most immigrant parents then take it one step further and wish their children to be the best in their chosen field. But my dad took a different turn—he wanted me to stay in balanced mediocrity.

In my dad's eyes, mediocrity was where happiness thrived. A solid pension plan with just enough money to pay the mortgage and go on a week-long vacation once a year was all you needed. It was a sign of success. The story that began to cement in my head was, any more, and you were asking for a life of isolation and the people you loved to start resenting you.

And the media pushed this narrative as well.

For example, *The Devil Wears Prada*, one of my favorite movies, showed a woman in a power position with a personal life that was going to hell.

All around me, there was evidence that I could either have the perfect family life filled with love and happiness or be successful in my job. There wasn't an option where I could do both.

And while my father's words and media depictions were etched in my brain, I continued to climb the corporate ladder. I couldn't find happiness in mediocrity, and I thought perhaps they were wrong. Maybe I'd find happiness in the promotions at work.

But *all of us* were wrong.

It was wrong to assume happiness was mediocrity, and I was wrong in assuming happiness was in top corporate positions.

Happiness is in finding new ways to expand upon your existing happiness.

Comfortable Misery

As I did some serious soul searching, I realized my contentment was in constant growth. I am happiest when I find new ways to expand upon my existing happiness.

I try to explain it like this: When you devour an incredible meal to the point where your stomach feels so big it feels like it could burst, you decline anything else because you're completely satisfied. But you know in a few hours you're going to be hungry again.

I love getting to the point of complete satisfaction and having new experiences and then digesting to the point where I want to do it again.

That's what Los Angeles gave me.

I arrived in L.A. without my family to throw my sister and her husband the baby shower for their first child. I stayed for two weeks—the longest I had ever been without my husband and children. And purely because I didn't have the distraction of caring for my own tiny humans, I was able to devote my time and energy to connecting with my sister, my brother-in-law, and my mother in ways we hadn't in years.

I met their friends; these incredible, inspiring creatives. So young, and successful, and people of color. I know that might sound strange, but I had been living twenty-four seven in the company of white success for so long that I didn't realize how foreign Black success had become to my world.

And being around it? I felt different. Free. Unmasked. Unguarded. Like I was finally releasing an exhale I'd been holding on to for ten years.

When I got back to Canada, I tried to explain it to my husband. I couldn't articulate it fully. All I knew was that something had shifted.

Four weeks later, we returned as a family, and the shift suddenly took hold of him as well. Every day of sun, every new experience, was like watching the light turn on inside him. We explored, we dreamed, and eventually, we stepped inside a house that made us say: *This. This is the life we can see for ourselves. This is where our kids can grow up. This is where memories will be made. I want more of this.*

And that's what scared me.

Because I knew what would happen next. We'd return to Toronto. The comfort of reality would set in. The fantasy would be folded up and stored in the "nice to think about" drawer.

What would our life look like six months from now if we changed nothing? I knew the answer. I knew what job I'd have, how we'd spend our summer. And I knew that even though I'd tasted something different—something better—I'd be tempted to stay right where I was.

Because that's what comfortable misery does.

I eventually realized I wanted to leave corporate, move to L.A., and build a purpose-filled career in coaching and working alongside my sister. But even though it was my dream, the limiting beliefs came flooding in: We can't ruin our kids' lives. It would be too expensive to move. We just put in a pool. How could we walk away now?

I clung to the comfort of our fine life. My dad's voice echoed in my ear with every conversation about getting serious about the move.

Sure, L.A. was the manifestation of exactly what I wanted. But could I do it? At least in Canada, I was comfortable. Miserable but comfortable.

And if I'm being honest, I *liked* complaining. The exasperated sighs. The sympathetic back rubs. The satisfaction of shooting down other people's solutions because I needed everyone to see how hard I had it.

When you give in to your limiting beliefs, there's no other feeling like the momentary bliss of complaining. You get to play victim to your circumstances. You get to believe everything is out of your control.

Even when doors open and people encourage you, it can feel easier to complain about not getting what you want than to find the courage to go after it. It's self-sabotage. A way to avoid rejection or the possibility that you're not good enough for what you're aiming for.

And I'll let you in on a secret: I still give in to those beliefs sometimes. Even as a coach who helps people break free from limiting beliefs, I haven't completely shed the idea that it's greedy to want more.

Limiting beliefs are ingrained in us. They show up, especially when we stretch into new spheres of uncertainty. The difference now is that I have tools to recognize them. I've learned that thoughts like these are a normal part of the process.

Because at the end of the day, we attempt to ignore the pull for more and cling to the false sense of security of "enough." And it's neuroscience.

The Neuroscience of Enough

Back in 2010, a study found that the sweet spot for financial happiness was an annual income of around $US75,000.

This was the point where your basic needs and even a few luxuries are comfortably covered. If we adjust for inflation, we could bump that figure up by $10,000 today and call it the "magic number" for "enough." But let's pause for a moment. What does "enough" actually mean when you consider how our brains are wired?

Think about the promotion you worked so hard for, the dream house you've pictured yourself in, or that new car you thought would be life changing. Maybe it was a relationship you believed would make you feel whole. At one point, you tied your sense of happiness and fulfillment to these goals, didn't you? And sure, when you reached them, it felt incredible—exciting, validating, even euphoric. But after a while, that excitement faded. Those milestones became part of your everyday routine, your new "normal."

This is what psychologists call hedonic adaptation (or the "hedonic treadmill"). It's the idea that no matter what big changes happen, good or bad, we tend to return to a baseline level of happiness. As you achieve goals or earn more money, your expectations rise too, leaving you chasing the next thing without feeling permanently satisfied.

Before long, those initial "wins" are followed by nagging questions: *What's next? How do I top this? Is this all there is?* As ambitious people, it's natural for us to want more. Our survival instincts push us to secure basic needs like food and shelter (extrinsic motivators), but our brains also crave deeper fulfillment, driven by something else entirely: intrinsic motivators. These types of motivators are the things that genuinely excite and inspire us, with or without external rewards.

So, what lights you up? What would you spend your time doing if there were no expectations? What's the activity that makes hours pass like minutes and leaves you thinking, *More of this, please*?

For high achievers, intrinsic motivators often center around three key areas:

- **Personal Growth:** Achieving something you once thought was out of reach. Whether it's learning a new skill or tackling a challenge, that rush of dopamine you feel when you hit a growth milestone is your brain's way of saying, *Yes. Keep going!*

- **Meaningful Relationships:** Building connections with people who resonate with your journey or help you grow in new ways. When you form deep bonds, your brain releases oxytocin, often called the "love hormone," reminding you how vital social connections are to your well-being.

- **Making a Difference:** Over time, all the knowledge and experiences you've gained create a natural desire to give back. Whether it's mentoring, volunteering, or simply lending a hand, these acts of service light up your brain's reward system, reinforcing the deep satisfaction that comes from helping others and fostering a sense of community.

Understanding and leaning into your intrinsic motivators isn't just important; it's life changing.

I wish I'd realized this ten years ago when I was struggling to understand why external successes weren't enough. I kept hitting milestones that should have felt fulfilling, but they didn't. I needed something more personal, something tied to who I really was. Looking back, I can see how much I thrived when I was learning new leadership skills, helping others grow, and creating connections that mattered. If I'd embraced those intrinsic motivators sooner, I could've saved myself so much guilt and self-doubt. Instead of second-guessing my ambitions, I might've started building the life I wanted sooner.

Putting It into Practice

Before you can define what enough looks like in this season of your life, you need to reconnect with what fuels you. With what makes you feel most alive and most yourself.

Take a moment. Think back to a time when you felt most energized, most in your skin, most aligned with who you are at your core. Maybe it was a particular chapter of your life, a specific experience, or even just a fleeting period where things felt right.

Describe that time in as much detail as you can conjure up. Where were you? What were you doing? Who were you with? How did you feel?

Your reflection:

List out all the things you were doing during that time. Use action words—*ing* words—that capture what filled you up.

(Examples: *learning, creating, mentoring, traveling, exploring, connecting, building, teaching, leading, writing, collaborating*)

Your words:

Choose five to seven of those words that bring you the most energy just reading them.

Your energizing words:

1.

2.

3.

4.

5.

6.

7.

Which of these words are absent from your life right now or showing up less than you'd like?

Your reflection:

What does this tell you? What might you need to bring more of into your life? What might you need to do less of?

Your insight:

Brainstorm: How can you bring more of these words— these actions, these energies—back into your life? Think small, realistic steps.

(Examples: Join a local writing group. Schedule time each week for exploring. Volunteer to mentor someone.)

Your ideas:

Receipts

Proof that you're not asking for too much—you're finally asking the right questions.

In this chapter, you didn't just read about redefining success—you confronted what "enough" has *actually* looked like in your life, and why it's never really satisfied you. Let's break down what you just did:

You told the truth.

- You named the quiet dissatisfaction that's been simmering under the surface.

- You acknowledged the tension between what you've achieved and what you *actually* want.

- You realized that "grateful" doesn't have to mean "silent and stuck."

You faced the voices.

- The inner critic. The cultural scripts. The family narratives.

- You identified the beliefs that told you wanting more made you selfish, ungrateful, or disloyal.

- And you gave yourself permission to question those voices instead of obeying them.

You named your fuel.

- You reconnected with what *actually* energizes you— those moments where you felt most alive, aligned, and *you*.

- You translated those moments into powerful action words.

- You identified what's missing right now, and you started mapping out how to bring those energies back into your daily life.

You cracked the code on "enough."

- You recognized the neuroscience behind your craving for more—and saw it not as greed, but growth.

- You shifted your focus from external validation to internal fulfillment.

- You stopped apologizing for your ambition and started listening to it instead.

Your Next Move

This week, take time to reconnect with what truly lights you up—the work, the ideas, the dreams that spark something real inside you. Not what looks good on paper. Not what impresses others. What energizes you.

And as you do, remind yourself: Enough was never meant to be a ceiling. It isn't about settling or shrinking to fit the room you're in. Enough is about expansion. It's about alignment. It's about building or entering rooms where you can show up as your fullest, most authentic self, and where your light doesn't have to dim to make others comfortable, especially those who think you should just be grateful for where you are and what you've got.

I'm grateful
for what I have
and I'm ready
for what's next

#BeInTheRoom

Chapter Three

Stop Being so Damn Grateful! Ask for the Steak!

"You get what you get and you don't get upset!"

If you've ever been around toddlers (or tried to keep one from melting down in a Target aisle), you know that line. It was basically my mantra when my kids were younger. I'd slave over a hot stove, or more accurately, scramble some eggs, and be met with groans because they wanted pancakes instead. And while their whiny entitlement grated my last nerve, I also kind of admired the audacity.

They didn't care what I sacrificed or how long I stood in the kitchen. They knew what they wanted, and weren't afraid to say it.

Case in point: I once sent my daughter to a neighbor's house for a playdate. When I came to pick her up, the mom sheepishly apologized.

"I'm so sorry. I didn't have proper food prepared for her lunch."

I was confused. My daughter didn't have allergies. She wasn't gluten-free, vegan, or on a juice cleanse. This is a child who once tried to eat a bar of soap. Let that sink in.

Then came the punch line.

"I offered her a grilled cheese sandwich, and she said, 'Actually, I'd prefer steak.'"

At first, I was mortified. I imagined this poor woman thinking we serve filet mignon like we were hosting Michelin-star brunches on weekdays. I almost died of secondhand embarrassment.

But underneath the panic, I was...impressed.

My five-year-old daughter looked at a plate of grilled cheese and asked—without hesitation—for *steak*. Not because she thought she'd get it, but because that's what she *wanted*. She had no concept of *"you should just be grateful."* No filter telling her to play it safe. Just unfiltered, delusional confidence that the world might say yes.

And honestly, my mind was blown.

Now here's the part that stings: That same daughter, now a teenager, has trouble asking for *anything* she wants. She hesitates and studies my face for a flicker of disapproval before she even finishes her sentence. Somewhere between grilled cheese and high school, she learned the lesson society (and parents) teaches all of us—especially girls:

Be grateful for what you're given. Don't ask for more. Don't make people uncomfortable. Don't seem greedy.

And we internalize that message so early, we don't even realize it's running the show.

And no, I'm *not* saying we should raise a generation of steak-demanding monsters. But I *am* saying that maybe

61

we've confused gratitude with obedience, with settling, even with silence.

You can be grateful and *still* want more. You can appreciate what's on your plate and still have the audacity to say, *"Actually, I'd prefer steak."*

And if a five-year-old can do it with that much clarity and confidence, what's stopping you?

You're Not Greedy for Wanting More

The idea of greed ties right into the illusion of "enough" (which we just chatted about in the last chapter) and the limits we set for ourselves. That constant pull for more can feel like a slippery slope you're barely able to keep your footing on. I know firsthand. Taking the leap into coaching was terrifying. I worried about collapsing my family's stability, but I went for it anyway.

And guess what? I wasn't alone.

So many of us, especially people of color, wrestle with this. We've accomplished more than we ever imagined, maybe even more than those who came before us, yet we still silence that inner voice whispering, *"What if there's more?"*

If you've been raised in a culture where survival was prioritized over self-actualization, this fear of wanting more isn't just personal, it's generational. It's not that you're ungrateful. It's that you were taught that gratitude was your shield against instability, being seen, and being punished.

The Eight Fears We Don't Say Aloud

Maybe you'll recognize a few of these:

1. **Fear of Greed:** *Is it greedy of me to want more? Am I a bad person for not being content with what I have? Will wanting more make me lose sight of what really matters?*

2. **Cultural and Religious Norms:** *In my culture or faith, humility and contentment are virtues. Does yearning for more contradict my beliefs? Am I going against the values I was raised with?*

3. **Deprivation of Others:** *If I take up more space, am I taking it away from someone else who deserves it? Does my pursuit of "more" mean that someone else gets "less"?*

4. **Social Comparison:** *Everyone around me is struggling; how can I justify wanting more? Wouldn't it be insensitive or tone deaf of me to strive for more when others have so little?*

5. **Self-Worth:** *Do I even deserve more? There are people who are more talented or work harder than me; why should I expect more for myself?*

6. **Fear of Judgment:** *If I reach for more and fail, will people think less of me? Will they label me as ungrateful or say, "I told you so"?*

7. **Family Expectations:** *My family sacrificed so much for me to be where I am. Would wanting more disappoint them or make them feel like their efforts were not enough?*

8. **Unrealistic Aspirations:** *The world seems to celebrate constant hustle and ambition. Can I even*

keep up? And if I do, will I end up perpetuating a cycle of never being satisfied?

How many of the above did you check off?

The first step in breaking down the psychological barriers that stop us from pursuing more in life is recognizing and addressing these conversations. When we acknowledge these fears and conflicts, we can begin dismantling them and free ourselves for what we truly desire and deserve.

The Gratitude Mistake

I was talking with a client—we'll call her Sylvia—and she brought up something I hear a lot, this idea that gratitude means you shouldn't want more. She told me she practiced gratitude regularly and felt like appreciating what she had meant she shouldn't want anything beyond it. But here's the thing—saying, *"Just be grateful,"* is not gratitude. It's scarcity thinking in disguise. And she's not alone in thinking that.

Gratitude isn't about just settling for what you have. It's about recognizing and valuing what you have while building toward what's next. It's the foundation, not the finish line. And this isn't just a nice-sounding mindset shift; it's actually backed by neuroscience.

Our brains operate in two main modes, a threat state and a reward state, which shape how we think, feel, and make decisions. Let's break that down.

When our brain is in threat state, it's operating under a primal survival mechanism, continuously scanning our environment for potential danger. When it detects a threat, the brain triggers what psychologist Daniel Goleman calls an "amygdala hijack." This reaction means the amygdala, the part of the brain responsible for emotional processing, overrides the prefrontal cortex, the center for rational thought. In other words, our brain goes into crisis mode, drawing energy and resources away from rational thought into self-preservation.

This hijack gets the body ready for a fight-or-flight response, making immediate survival the focus and often dampening our capacity for long-term planning and openness to change.

Contrast that with the reward state, which is characterized by a sense of safety and satisfaction. This state is a result of positive emotions and experiences, such as gratitude. When we acknowledge what we're thankful for, we train our brain to scan for what's working, instead of just what's missing. That shift tells our nervous system: *You're safe, you have options, now go create.*

This shift then activates the prefrontal cortex, which is associated with higher-order functions like creativity, strategic thinking, and problem solving. When we're in this state, it allows us to move beyond immediate concerns (and fears) and take on broader, more innovative perspectives.

In simplest terms, gratitude is more than a mere feel-good, check-the-box-for-my-morning-routine exercise; it is a transformative practice that helps transition your brain from its default state of protection and defensiveness to one that is reward oriented, risk taking, and expansive. Used as a tool in this way, gratitude can create an environment where being in the room becomes not just a possibility but a realistic reality. So don't stifle it with scarcity.

Your Brain on Gratitude

When we discuss gratitude, we use the term *practice* intentionally. It emphasizes how using gratitude to activate the reward state isn't an automatic response for us. It requires effort, sometimes a lot. But this practice is so important when it comes to counteracting our brain's default mode to scan our environment for threats and hyper-fixate on negatives.

Even though most of us don't face daily life-or-death threats like food scarcity or physical danger, our brains are still wired to be on high alert. You'd think that in a world where survival is more secure, especially in developed regions, we'd spend more time in a reward state, right?

Wrong!

Our minds are constantly scanning for anything that might threaten our progress, even when no real danger exists.

These days, our "threats" look different. They're not about outrunning predators but about navigating social, professional, and personal pressures. Fear of failure, social rejection, or not living up to our own expectations can feel just as intense. A comment from a boss, negative feedback online, or even a weird vibe from a friend can send us spiraling. And while those things might not seem as deadly as the physical dangers our ancestors faced, our brains don't know the difference.

Research backs this up. Naomi Eisenberger, a leading social neuroscience researcher at UCLA, conducted an interesting study on social rejection. Her team used a computer game called Cyberball to simulate exclusion while monitoring participants' brain activity with MRI scans. The results? Our brains process social rejection in a way that's eerily similar to physical pain.[4]

But what does that mean for how we handle stress today?

The Cyberball experiment was basically a digital version of playground exclusion. Participants thought they were playing an online ball-tossing game with two other people. At first, everything seemed fair. Everyone got a turn. But then, without warning, the other "players" stopped passing them the ball, tossing it only to each other instead.

Here's the twist: Those other players weren't real. It was all part of the experiment. But even after learning that, participants still reported feeling hurt, rejected, and even angry, just as if they had been snubbed in real life. It's a reminder that our brains aren't good at distinguishing actual and perceived rejection. The emotional impact is always real.

The MRI scans showed that people who reported feeling most rejected had the highest levels of activity in the part of the brain tied to the emotional component of pain, or what's often known as the "suffering" aspect of pain.

This study makes one thing super clear: Social rejection hurts, and our brains take it seriously. In a world where success (and, in many ways, survival) depends on belonging, being part of an "in group" isn't just about social perks; it gives us access to resources, protection, and opportunities.

---

4   Eisenberger, N. I., Lieberman, M. D., & Williams, K. D. (2003). *Does rejection hurt? An fMRI study of social exclusion.* Science, 302(5643), 290-292. https://www.sciencemag.org/content/302/5643/290.full.pdf

The hard part is, without even really trying, we're constantly feeding our brain with new and ongoing data that keeps us in a perpetual state of fearing rejection.

Think about how much time we spend tuned into society. Social media, news cycles, and constant comparison creates a sense of urgency that isn't always real but feels like it is. It sounds like:

"Everyone else is so much further ahead than me. I'm falling behind."

"What's the point of even trying when the world is going to shit?"

"If I'm not online, I'll miss out."

So of course we're stressed! But here's the good news— while our brains are wired to focus on threats, we can shift our mindset toward a reward state. And no, this isn't about toxic positivity or pretending everything is fine. Practicing gratitude doesn't mean ignoring challenges. It means giving yourself the mental space to approach them with creativity, strategy, and resilience.

This is why gratitude, when used right, isn't about pretending everything's okay. It's about creating enough inner safety to keep moving forward, even when rejection is real.

Put It into Practice

Let's channel your inner steak-loving toddler.

The reason most of us don't ask for steak is because somewhere along the way, we were told grilled cheese is *plenty*—and to even want more was rude, greedy, or unrealistic. But today, we're unlearning that noise.

Take a moment to get radically honest with yourself:

What are you settling for that you've been pretending to be grateful for?

It could be a job, a client, a salary, a relationship, a team dynamic, or even your own pace. Write it down. No judgment, just truth.

Your response:

If you could have exactly what you wanted, what would you actually ask for?

Now's not the time to shrink. Don't just wish for "a little more flexibility" if what you really want is full autonomy. Don't ask for "a seat at the table" when you secretly want to *run the whole damn boardroom.*

Say the steak.

Your response:

What story are you telling yourself about why you can't ask for more?

Go deeper: Is it about being seen as ungrateful? Is it a cultural or family narrative? Are you afraid of what it would mean about you if someone said no? Unpack it. Drag it into the light.

Your response:

Write your "and" statement.

Try this reframe:

"I'm grateful for [insert current reality] **and** I desire [insert your bold ask]."

Example:

"I'm grateful for my role leading this team and I desire to build a business where my impact isn't capped by someone else's vision."

"I'm grateful for the opportunities I've had and I desire more visibility, more income, and more influence."

Your response:

Now say it out loud. Yes, out loud.

Bonus points if you say it while making grilled cheese—just to remind yourself that settling is optional.

Want to deepen the shift? Use your "And" Statement as a daily mantra this week. Write it on a sticky note. Make it your phone background. Say it before every Zoom meeting. Repeat it until your brain believes you can want more *and* still be wildly grateful for where you are.

That's not greedy. That's alignment. And it's where your power lives.

Receipts

You've just unpacked the difference between gratitude and settling—and called bullshit on the belief that wanting more makes you ungrateful.

Here's what you've done (whether you realized it or not):

- You called out the stories and social conditioning that have kept you playing small—especially the belief that you should be satisfied with what you've been handed.

- You named the inner fears that usually stay buried— like the fear of greed, judgment, and disappointing others.

- You examined how your brain responds to threat vs. reward, and how practicing gratitude (real gratitude) isn't about playing it safe—it's about creating internal safety so you can stretch.

- You saw how subtle messages—from family, culture, and even your own nervous system—have shaped your idea of what's possible.

- You learned that gratitude is not the opposite of ambition. It's the fuel for it.

And most importantly:

- You practiced *saying the steak*. You gave yourself permission to name what you *actually* want—even if it feels audacious. Even if it makes someone uncomfortable. Even if it's more than you were taught to ask for.

- You've stopped confusing "gratitude" with "good behavior."

- You've started choosing expansion over obedience.

- You're no longer performing contentment. You're building alignment.

Your Next Move

As you begin to embrace gratitude and allow yourself to want more, I know the voice that creeps in next. The one that whispers, *What if I fail?* The one that urges you to stay small, to stay safe, to stay unseen.

But here's the truth: That voice will follow you into every new room you enter. It's not a sign that you're not ready—it's a sign that you're growing. That you're standing at the edge of something bigger.

The next step in this journey is to face that voice head-on. Not to silence it completely, but to recognize it for what it is:

fear trying to protect you in the only way it knows how. And then, to choose your *hard* with intention. Because staying where you are is hard. Stretching into who you're meant to be is hard. The question is: Which hard moves you closer to the room where you truly belong?

Choose your hard

#BeInTheRoom

Chapter Four

Too Many F-Words – Fear, Failure, and Finding Your Way Forward

Fear Has Cost Me Money, Peace, Time—and Nearly My Dream.

Despite being someone who coaches others through it, fear, especially the fear of failure, has not only caused me anxiety but physically held me back from going after what I want. If I'm being honest, it still does to this day. It's funny how a state of mind can have such tangible consequences.

When I decided to get serious about moving to California, the fear of failure delayed and limited the plan. To me, failure meant not being able to give my kids the life they were accustomed to in Canada. If my husband and I couldn't maintain the same quality of life, I would feel that our inability to provide and our kids' distress and unhappiness were my failures.

No matter how many times he would reassure me that we were in it together, I was convinced that it wouldn't be our failure as parents—it would be *my* failure alone. Our disastrous life would be the result of my selfish actions. I was the one taking the income hit and starting from scratch.

My husband was fortunate; his company operated in both Canada and the U.S., making his transition seamless. It was me who was forced to prove myself and find a way back to the thriving financial state I'd once achieved.

So, when I ask you to imagine doing the scary thing right now, I know how terrifying the thought can be. Whether it's booking a solo trip, signing up for a race, or accepting a new job, I can relate to your fears.

But I don't just want you to sit with that fear. That feeling. That emotion. I want you to name it. Acknowledge it. Move through it versus over or from it.

Emotions Run the Show—Even in Your Corner Office

"I'm so sorry. I didn't think I'd cry in this session."

I hear this all the time. Executives, entrepreneurs, creatives, and leaders come to a coaching call ready to take control of their future. They show up with blazers on, notebooks open, pen in hand, ready to jot down tactical steps and action items that will help them get unstuck.

At first, it feels familiar and safe—we're making plans, setting goals, mapping strategy. But somewhere between minute ten and fifteen, the shift happens. Emotions bubble up. The very feelings they've worked so hard to contain start to rise to the surface. And almost always, the apology comes: *"I know this isn't therapy. I didn't mean to get emotional."*

What most people don't realize, especially in high-stakes, high-performing environments, is this:

Emotion drives 80 to 90% of our decisions. Yes, even in boardrooms. Even in spreadsheets. Even in your most "rational" moments.

And I know how counterintuitive that sounds.

You've been taught your whole life that leadership means logic. That strength looks like stoicism. That the best decisions come from leaving your emotions at the door.

But the truth is you can't leave behind what lives in your brain.

Emotions reside in the limbic system, the part of the brain responsible for instinct, memory, and emotional processing. That system is *always* online. It operates automatically— meaning your emotions are shaping your reactions, assessments, and decisions whether you acknowledge them or not.

And yet many of us have been conditioned to suppress, ignore, or outthink those emotions, especially in professional spaces. But suppressing emotions doesn't make them go away. It just makes them unconscious drivers, pulling strings behind the scenes while we pretend logic is running the show.

It's like calling a board meeting to decide the future of your company, and failing to invite the majority stakeholder.

Emotions are not the enemy of good decision making. They are the informants.

They tell you where your values live. They signal when something feels off. They reveal what you're truly afraid of, what you deeply desire, and what matters most, even if you're not ready to admit it out loud.

And when we refuse to acknowledge that inner world? When we bury our emotional intelligence under layers of "professionalism"? That's when we start making decisions that are misaligned, shortsighted, or driven by fear dressed up as logic.

Here's what neuroscience tells us:

- Emotions are neurologically linked to decision making. People with damage to the emotional centers of their brain struggle to make even basic decisions, despite having intact reasoning ability.

- The amygdala and limbic brain send emotional data before your rational brain even kicks in. So by the time you're "thinking it through," your gut has already weighed in.

- Emotional suppression increases cognitive load, which actually makes your decision making less efficient—not more.

So no, emotions aren't weakness. They are data. Direction. Leverage.

The goal isn't to be run by them—but to run *with* them.

You don't have to become emotionally indulgent. But you do have to become emotionally intelligent.

Because once you name what's really going on internally, you stop making decisions based on fear, shame, or false stories—and start leading from a place of clarity, power, and self-trust.

It's already running the show. You might as well give it a seat at the table.

The Cover Story Trap

I'm afraid of failure makes for a great headline, but it's not the actual story.

Let me tell you about Stacey.

Stacey was an award-winning entertainer, a mother, a wife, and a new entrepreneur. From the outside, it looked like she was built to win at anything she set her mind to. But when it came to building her business, she kept getting stuck. When I asked what was holding her back, she said, *"I'm afraid of failing."*

But I've learned not to stop at the first answer. Fear of failure is what I call a cover story. It's the explanation that feels safe to say out loud. But underneath? There's usually something much deeper.

Through our work together, Stacey uncovered what was really happening. She didn't feel fear of failure—she felt inadequate. Nervous. Exposed. All those years of being directed by managers, agents, and teams had left her doubting her own ideas. She'd been told to stay in her lane so many times that she no longer trusted her own voice. And every time she abandoned a project, it reinforced the story in her head: *Your ideas aren't good enough.*

The tears that came weren't weakness. They were clarity. She could finally see the rope around her ankle that had been holding her in place. And once she could see it, she could start to untie it.

But the thing is, the fear of failure (or fear of success) is almost never the real issue. It's the shiny surface layer that hides something harder to say out loud.

We lean on that cover story for a few reasons:

- It simplifies complex emotions into something easier to explain.

- It shields us from deeper feelings like shame or unworthiness.

- It helps us feel like we're in control of our narrative.

- It distracts us from the harder inner work of self-exploration.

- It keeps the status quo intact so we don't have to confront big, scary changes.

- It externalizes the problem, making it about outcomes instead of internal worth.

But if you want to move forward, you have to get beneath the cover story. You have to name what's really going on. Because once you name it, you can tame it.

There's a phrase in neuroscience I love, "name it to tame it," coined by Dr. Daniel J. Siegel, a clinical professor of psychiatry at the UCLA School of Medicine and the founding co-director of the Mindful Awareness Research Center at UCLA.

The phrase suggests that when you label an emotion, you activate the rational part of your brain—the prefrontal cortex—that helps you manage and regulate the fear response coming from the amygdala. It's like putting the brakes on an emotional hijack so you can think clearly and act intentionally.

But how do you name what you're feeling when all you can articulate is "fear"?

That's where tools like the Feelings Wheel come in. Created by Dr. Gloria Willcox, it helps break down big, broad emotions into more precise language. Instead of just "afraid," maybe what you're really feeling is insecure, inadequate, or vulnerable. The more specific you can get, the easier it becomes to address the real issue.

For Stacey, using this approach changed everything. Once she could see that it wasn't failure she feared—it was trusting herself—she could focus on building that trust. She could take action from a place of clarity rather than confusion.

So, if you find yourself stuck, if you're telling yourself you're afraid of failing, I invite you to dig deeper and name what's really there. Because when you do, you take the first step toward reclaiming your power, even though it's hard.

Choose Your Hard

Amanda was burning out behind her red-framed glasses. A top attorney at a prestigious firm, she looked like the picture of success. But on our first Zoom call, she was barely holding it together.

It was our first session and the reason she was here was clear: She was at a crossroads.

Like so many of my clients, she was seeking a different life, a better one. A life of self-employment and total control over finances and time. Her choice was seemingly straightforward: resign now to pursue her entrepreneurial dream or stay six more months to secure her bonus. On the surface level, the logical choice appeared to be the one where she waited, building her business on the side while enjoying the financial comfort of a lawyer's pay with a hefty bonus coming relatively soon.

But her shaky voice and desperate tone hinted at a deeper struggle. From her arms across her chest to the deep crease between her eyebrows, Amanda looked desperate for another option as we discussed the "logical" choice.

"Let's pretend you decided to leave your job early to pursue your consulting business? What challenges would you face?" I asked.

"Financial instability." Amanda picked at the skin around her thumbnail. *"And I don't have the experience to run a business, so I'd probably fail."* She rattled off the challenges instantly. She'd clearly been thinking of them for some time.

Fears and challenges of change were always easy to name.

I shifted the focus of the conversation. *"And tell me about the challenges you'll face if you stay at the law firm for an extra six months."*

Amanda's eyes instantly filled with tears, her mouth pulled downward, and she looked away from the camera. *"Every day—"* She sniffed and reached for some tissues off camera and balled them in her fist, wiping her eyes and nose.

"Take your time," I said.

"Every day, I dread going to work. It's isolating; I'm one of the few Black women in the firm, and the microaggressions are constant. And I think I'm even becoming depressed." Fat tears rolled down her cheeks. She didn't bother trying to wipe them away now. *"I'm going to see a therapist about it*

next week, but I don't have the energy I once did for life. I don't care about work, and I'm constantly on edge."

I looked at this successful Black woman before me with new eyes. Her choice wasn't simply between the easy path of staying and the hard path of leaving. It was a decision between two different types of hardship. The so-called "easy" option of staying was, in fact, eroding her well-being and sense of self, making it far from easy in the true sense of the word.

You're Already in the Hard

Before we continue with Amanda's story, I want you to focus on you for a moment: Imagine your life is precisely the same one year from now.

In twelve months, you're in the same job, making the same amount, living where you are currently, and experiencing the same longing for something different.

Nothing's changed.

How does that make you feel?

I'm willing to bet that you have a tightness in your chest, maybe an uneasy twist in your stomach.

Does the prospect of the exact same life feel disappointing?

If so, you're on the wrong path and occupying the wrong rooms.

Staying in a place of unhappiness and dissatisfaction does everyone around you a disservice. From your family members to your colleagues and friends, but especially yourself. When you are in a place that lacks inspiration or drains your energy, it impacts your moods and even your actions. You might become more hostile to those around you, dragging them down into a state of misery so you're not alone in your darkness. Not to mention, your quality of work will likely suffer as well.

The reality is that no matter what you decide to do, it's going to be *so* fucking hard.

People say, *"Choose a job you love, and you'll never work a day in your life,"* but what they don't tell you is that no matter what direction you decide to take, it's going to be hard. Whether you stay in your current position or take a leap of faith and start something new, I can promise you breakdowns will be abundant, tears and snot will flow, you'll want to bang your head against the wall more times than you can count, and you'll question every decision you've made up until that point.

(Okay, I know this sounds bleak. Stay with me, I promise it gets better.)

So, what's the answer? Are we just doomed to live unhappily no matter which path we choose?

Not if you choose the hard that makes it worth it.

But what does that mean? Isn't the only "hard" option the one with the unknown outcome? Staying in your current situation can't possibly be as hard as diving headfirst into a new path, right?

We often trick ourselves into believing that staying in the same miserable situation is the easier path. Our brains seek out easy. They gravitate toward easy more than they might gravitate toward hard. But it's a trick. On the surface level, one option might seem easier, but it's tough either way.

This life that you're currently in, the one where you're unhappy and miserable, is not easy. Not only are you already dissatisfied and unmotivated to excel on your current path, but a year from now, you're going to feel worse. You'll be disappointed and regretful, consumed by distress, wishing you'd made the jump earlier because at least you'd be out of the situation you're in now.

You'll scold yourself for not choosing to push past your fear of failure because at least you'd have some answers as to whether it might work out or not instead of ruminating over the "what could have been" sentiments. By staying, by choosing the pseudo-easy path, you're going to feel a level of despair, unfulfillment, and resentment. Those are not easy feelings to have. They are crippling and impact your overall satisfaction in life. So, you're not choosing between an easy and a hard; you're choosing between two hards.

How do we choose which hard to pursue? You look at your options and choose the hard that bends your life in the direction of who you're becoming and the life you're building.

Every time you find yourself thinking, *Oh, I don't want to do that,* or *That feels uncomfortable,* ask yourself, *What is the hard I'm choosing?*

I walked away from a secure corporate job to build a business that aligned with my purpose and values, and let's be real, it hasn't been all sunshine and passive income.

There have been nights I've stared at the ceiling, spiraling over where the next chunk of money would come from. Days I've posted content and immediately wanted to crawl under a rock. The emotional whiplash of constantly putting myself out there is *real*.

But then I remember: **This is the hard I chose.**

Sure, it might seem easier to go back to a job where the paycheck hits like clockwork. Where someone else defines the metrics of success and foots the bill for my professional development. But that life? That version of "easy"? It was hard in a whole different way.

It meant shrinking and settling.

So I chose *this* hard: the hard that stretches me into the woman I'm here to become, the work I'm meant to do, and the impact I'm here to make.

The Formula for Change and Amanda's Decision

Once you identify which hard you want to choose, the question of *"Am I strong enough to actually choose the hard that brings me in the direction of where I want to be?"* comes up.

Here's the good news: There's a formula to figure that out.

Wishy-washy motivational quotes and advice don't work for a lot of people. And I can tell you firsthand how they tend to fall short with those in more technical, high-pressure, and demanding careers, like those in the medical and legal fields.

Amanda was one of those people who needed concrete, tangible advice to even begin to dig herself out of her pit of despair.

And I had just the thing: the formula for change.

The formula for change, often written as D x V x F > R, represents a model for understanding what it takes for people to truly choose the hard that comes with change. It stands for Dissatisfaction x Vision x Action > Resistance. This formula was originally assembled by Richard Beckhard and David Gleicher and further developed by Kathie Dannemiller. We most often see it in the field of organizational development and change management to assess and enhance the effectiveness of change initiatives within organizations, but I've found that it's also highly effective for determining the costs and benefits of personal change.

This isn't just math. It's the moment everything starts to make sense.

Let's break it down further and see how we can apply it to your life, like I did for Amanda:

D stands for dissatisfaction or the level of discomfort with your current situation. Without a high enough level of dissatisfaction, there's little motivation to initiate change.

V represents the vision or the desired outcome that we hope to achieve. A clear and compelling vision helps to provide direction and focus during sometimes tumultuous times of change.

F is for first steps or the specific actions that need to be taken to initiate change. Breaking down the process into manageable steps can make the change feel less daunting and more achievable.

Finally, *R* stands for resistance, or the forces that hinder your progress toward change. These resistors can look like fear, complacency, or simply a lack of resources.

Notice that the *R* stands alone on the right side of the equation, and that's intentional because of just how powerful it has the potential to be. In both me and my clients, I see the same top resistors to change over and over. Fear is a big one—fear of the unknown, fear of failure, and even fear of success can all hold us back from embracing change. Another resistor is complacency, or the tendency to stick with the status quo because it's comfortable and familiar. Lack of resources, such as time, money, or support, can also make it difficult to enact change.

Once you plug in your unique variables, what does this formula tell us? It suggests that successful change can only happen when your dissatisfaction with your current state, coupled with a clear vision of the future and concrete, achievable actions to reach that vision, is greater than your resistance to change.

By recognizing and addressing your resistors, you can begin to unlock the power of the formula for change and choose the hard that creates meaningful change in our lives and communities.

Amanda, the lawyer from the beginning of this chapter, took this formula and applied it to her own life. She analyzed the data, weighed the variables, and made the decision to resign from the law firm the next day.

That's right, she quit her job less than twenty-four hours after our conversation.

It was a brave step toward a future aligned with her aspirations and well-being. It underscored the importance of considering the "hard" aspects in both options, not just in terms of immediate challenges, but in terms of long-term impact and personal fulfillment. By looking beyond the surface-level ease of staying, she recognized the deeper, more profound difficulty it posed to her future self.

At life's major crossroads, it's essential to weigh both the immediate and future hardships. Sometimes, the path that seems more challenging initially can lead to greater satisfaction and alignment with our deeper values and goals.

You're already doing something hard. Wouldn't you rather it be worth it?

Put It into Practice:

If you're stuck at a crossroads, paralyzed by fear of failure, or unsure whether to stay or leap, it's time to bring clarity to what's really driving your decision.

The formula for change (D x V x F > R) helps you see whether your desire for change outweighs your resistance. This exercise will help you fill in those variables with honesty and precision.

Name your dissatisfaction

What's draining you, frustrating you, or making you long for something different?

Your reflection:

Deepen your understanding with the feelings wheel

A quick Google search will pull one up. What emotions are connected to this dissatisfaction? Look beyond fear or stress. Get specific. Are you feeling inadequate? Trapped? Overlooked? Disconnected?

Your words:

Articulate your vision

If your life looked and felt the way you want, what would be different? What would light you up?

Your reflection:

Identify your first steps

What small, tangible actions could move you toward that vision?

Your ideas:

Name your resistance

What's holding you back? Be honest. Fear of failure? Fear of success? Complacency? A need for external approval? Lack of resources?

Your reflection:

Weigh your equation

Based on what you've written, do your dissatisfaction, vision, and first steps feel stronger than your resistance? If not, where do you need to build strength—in your clarity, your plan, or your emotional readiness?

Your insight:

Choose your hard

What hard will you choose—the hard of staying where you are, or the hard of stepping toward change?

Your decision:

☐ The hard of staying the same

☐ The hard of change

Receipts

You didn't just read about fear—you stared it down. Here's what you walked away with:

- **You named your fear for what it really is.**

  - Not just fear of failure—but the deeper truths hiding underneath: insecurity, doubt, unworthiness, shame.

  - You looked beneath the cover story and put real language to the thing that's been holding you back.

- **You learned that emotion is not your enemy**

  - You now understand that 80 to 90% of your decisions are emotionally driven, and trying to suppress that doesn't make you strong, it makes you blind.

  - You reclaimed emotion as a source of clarity, not chaos.

  - You proved to yourself that logic and emotion can work together.

- **You chose your hard**

  - You stopped asking, *"Is this going to be hard?"* and started asking, *"Which hard is worth it?"* You made the powerful distinction between staying stuck and stepping forward—and committed to the hard that aligns with the future version of you.

- **You used a proven formula to assess your readiness**

  - You mapped your personal formula for change: Dissatisfaction × Vision × First Steps > Resistance

  - You saw the truth laid out in black and white—and discovered that your desire for more might finally be greater than your fear.

  - You moved beyond self-help fluff and into measurable self-awareness. You created a grounded framework to guide your next move, with both your heart and your head fully on board.

This chapter may have been the hardest one so far. It asked you to tell the truth about what you fear most, and who you could become if you moved anyway. But you did the work. And now?

You're still here. Stronger. Clearer. Braver.

Your Next Steps

In Part One, you didn't just flip through pages—you did foundational work that most people spend their whole lives avoiding.

You called out the invisible weight of success and named the unspoken pressures you've been carrying. You challenged the myth of "enough" and started defining success on your terms, not the ones handed down by systems, cultures, or expectations. You uncovered the fear narratives quietly running the show, and instead of letting them dictate your path, you chose your hard with intention and honesty. You've begun to see fear for what it really is—not a stop sign, but a signal. A signpost pointing toward the next level of your evolution.

But let's be clear: noticing the door isn't the same as walking through it.

Now we shift. From awareness to agency. From survival patterns to conscious power.

This next section is about shedding the old scripts, some of which you didn't even realize you were following. The ones that told you to stay small, stay safe, stay silent.

You'll learn how to rewrite those internalized stories with intention, so that your actions match your ambition, and your presence in every room reflects the truth of who you are, not the version others feel most comfortable with.

You've already begun the shift. Now, let's make it undeniable.

Part Two
Who Wrote This Script?

UNLEARNING THE STORIES THAT TOLD YOU TO SHRINK

My presence is
not an accident

#BeInTheRoom

Chapter Five

Stop Calling It Impostor Syndrome – It's Not You, It's the System

"I want to do X, but I have such impostor syndrome!"

I hear some version of this all the time. And every time, I flinch. Not because it's unfamiliar, but because of how casually we internalize something that should have been questioned all along.

Let's get something straight: Impostor syndrome isn't a diagnosis of a broken self. It's a symptom of a broken system. A system that rewards confidence over competence, that tells people (especially women of color and anyone at the margins) that their uncertainty is a personal failing rather than a predictable response to exclusion.

And let's pause for a moment to really think about that word: *syndrome.*

A syndrome, by definition, refers to a group of symptoms that consistently occur together, usually pointing to an underlying disease, disorder, or dysfunction within the individual. It implies that there's something wrong inside the person that needs to be diagnosed, treated, or fixed.

But that's not what's happening here. The feelings of doubt, fraudulence, or fear of exposure that we label impostor syndrome aren't signs of an internal disorder. They're logical human responses to external conditions; to environments where you're excluded, underestimated, or navigating double standards.

Calling it a syndrome shifts attention to the individual, as if the problem lies in you rather than in the system you're working so hard to survive.

And worse, it puts the burden of fixing the problem on the very person who's most impacted by it.

So let's stop calling it a syndrome.

I could tell you stories from clients who believed they had "the syndrome" or even shared my own. But what's the point? If you're resonating with this, you already know it's widespread. The question isn't *Do I have it?* It's *What's causing it?*

And more often than not, it's not you.

You're Not an Impostor. You're Just Scared.

Most people misuse the term impostor syndrome like it's some big, intimidating beast guarding the door to the next level of their life. But let's be honest: that's not impostor syndrome. That's just regular-ass self-doubt.

Real impostor syndrome doesn't show up before the opportunity. It shows up after you've said yes.

After the title. After the offer. After the win.

That's when the second-guessing starts. That's when the doubt whispers, *"Maybe they made a mistake."*

When the thought *Am I a fraud?* creeps in, I always come back to *Catch Me If You Can*, that Leo DiCaprio movie where he cons his way through life pretending to be a doctor, a lawyer, a pilot. You name it, he faked it. Not once did he have the right training or credentials. Just charm and boldness.

That is a fraud.

Leo's character would slide into the cockpit, throw on the uniform, and start using terms he learned in a pamphlet at the airport gift shop. He *should* have been escorted out.

But you?

You've done the work.

You've got the damn pilot's license.

You passed the exams.

You've logged the hours. You earned your seat.

You didn't fake your way in through charm and confidence. You earned your way in through capacity and courage.

And still, you're sitting there wondering if someone's going to find out you don't belong?

That's not fraud, that's a false narrative and fear. That's the residue of systems built to make you second-guess your power.

This chapter isn't going to be another rundown on impostor syndrome; that horse has been beaten to death. Instead, we're diving into the anatomy of self-doubt that simmers low and hot, especially in high achievers. And we're going to stop pathologizing what, in reality, is a rational response to systems that were never designed for you.

High Achievers and Self-Doubt

Here's the problem: High achievers aren't suffering from some personal defect. They're operating in performance-obsessed systems that teach us to fear failure, see value in output, and mistake external praise for self-worth.

The paradox is huge—people who overcome hurdles often wrestle with doubts about their worthiness for future wins. At first glance, it seems illogical, even ridiculous, which fuels the misconception that high achievers are immune to self-doubt. We idolize them, assuming that matching their achievements would make us feel more confident stepping into new opportunities. But this belief only reinforces the idea that our own self-doubt signals inadequacy for the future we want.

It's counterintuitive, but admiration can actually *intensify* self-doubt.

The higher the pedestal, the harder the fall—at least, that's the fear. The more people believe in you, the more terrifying it becomes to disappoint them. The pressure to perform and maintain an image of competence and success becomes intense. This pressure can amplify feelings of impostor syndrome, as high achievers may fear that taking on new challenges will expose their perceived shortcomings. The idea of falling short of others' expectations—or disappointing those who admire them—adds another layer of stress, making it even harder to step away from the façade of constant success.

Adam Grant, the organizational psychologist and author, offers an interesting perspective on this. He points out that many high achievers, particularly those who've been straight-A students (raising my hand here!), often develop an anxiety about maintaining their perfect streak. For these individuals, it's not just about a fear of failure; it's about avoiding situations where success isn't guaranteed. This can create a reluctance to explore new and unfamiliar areas, even when doing so could lead to growth.

Grant's insight isn't about flawed people; it's about how educated professional systems train us to perform within safe, linear paths. Straight As are great, but at what cost? These systems rarely reward curiosity, vulnerability, or risk, and without those things, how do we grow?

Grant explains that high achievers who are used to excelling in structured environments with set guidelines can become risk-averse. Their track record of success rarely allows for trial and error, and this means they may avoid challenges where their abilities are uncertain. This avoidance can limit learning and growth. For example, in the workplace, it might mean passing up new projects or leadership roles that push them outside their comfort zone—all because they're afraid of not excelling immediately.

I celebrate my children's 4.0 GPA. It's an incredible accomplishment. But I also wonder: What values does it teach them? Are they learning to chase curiosity, or just approval? Are they building the courage to fail, or just the fear of falling?

Sure, it's admirable to keep a perfect record, but it can simultaneously hold high achievers back. It can prevent new challenges and the opportunity to learn from mistakes.

Having a growth mindset rather than a perfectionist one is important. After all, true achievement comes from pushing boundaries, not just staying within them.

So let's name it for what it really is.

If you're doubting your place in the room, ask: Is this *really* a lack of confidence? Or is it a lack of representation, support, and psychological safety?

The doubt may feel personal, but the cause is often structural.

You are not the syndrome. You are the system's receipt.

Putting It into Practice

Self-doubt isn't the enemy. It's data—a voice trying to protect you. The key isn't to silence it, but to partner with it. To listen closely, examine what it's really saying, and decide what's worth addressing.

Let's walk through it.

Identify the voice

What's the self-doubt story playing in your mind right now?

(Example: *Who am I to lead this team?* or *Who am I to pitch this idea?*)

Your voice:

Look at the data. What (if anything) makes the statement <u>not</u> true?

List real, tangible evidence that shows you are capable. What experience, expertise, or qualities support your right to be here?

(Example: *I've led several projects to success. I have logged several hours in experience and education in this area.*)

Your evidence:

Where (if anywhere) is there a gap?

Sometimes self-doubt points to something useful—a skill you want to build, a connection you want to strengthen. Identify if there's an area you could grow to make your case to yourself undeniable.

(Example: *I've received feedback that I can improve my presentation skills. I do not have certifications in this area that's required.*)

Your gap (if any):

What can you do to mitigate that gap?

List small, achievable actions that help you close the gap or strengthen your foundation.

(Example: I can register for a class. I can have a conversation with someone in this role to get more clarity on what is required.)

Your next steps:

Reframe the voice.

Now, take your original statement of doubt and turn it into something true, affirming, and grounded in your evidence.

(Example: I am qualified to lead this team or project, and what I do not know, I will leverage resources to figure it out.)

Your new belief:

Receipts

Here's a recap of the truth you've claimed and the lies you've left behind.

- You've challenged the narrative that your uncertainty is a personal flaw,and named it instead as a rational response to systems designed without you in mind.

- You've separated self-doubt from shame.

- You've recognized that having questions doesn't make you an impostor. It makes you aware, discerning, and human.

- You've reclaimed the difference between being underprepared and being under-supported.

- You've acknowledged that confidence isn't a prerequisite to belonging.

- You've practiced partnering with self-doubt instead of trying to silence it—tuning into what it's trying to protect and deciding where you want to lead from.

- You've realized that fear at the next level isn't evidence you don't belong—it's evidence that you're expanding.

- You've shifted your story from *"I'm not enough"* to *"I'm already equipped, and I'm still evolving."*

- You've stopped asking permission to be in the room. You've started making space for your voice, your presence, and your impact.

- You've remembered: You are not the problem. You are the proof.

Your Next Move

As you start to challenge those doubts—as you name your strengths, list your wins, and claim your place—don't be surprised when another voice shows up.

The one that says, *"It's not that big of a deal."*

The one that whispers, *"Is that really a strength?"*

The one that leaves you questioning, *"Am I enough?"*

That voice thrives in the gap—the space between who you've been and who you are becoming.

That's where we're headed next. Because learning to be in the room isn't just about getting in—it's about surviving, thriving, and leading in the gap between the old you and the version of you that's ready to own the space.

Celebration is
strategy.
Not complacency.

#BeInTheRoom

Chapter Six

Don't Hold Your Applause – Reclaiming Progress in a World That Keeps Moving the Finish Line

It was a regular Tuesday afternoon when Robert and I met for one of our standing coaching calls. Just three months earlier, Robert had taken the leap so many dream about but few actually make: he left his high-paying corporate job and launched his own coaching firm. No major gigs lined up or formal coaching certifications. Just passion, experience, and a strong network to leverage.

And now? He was sharing the news that he'd landed a six-figure contract with a major airline—a contract that would've once felt like an impossible goal.

From the outside, it looked like he was there. He had done what he set out to do. He had left the security of a corporate paycheck, built something of his own, and secured work that validated his expertise at the highest level.

"Congrats on how far you've come," I told him, genuinely thrilled at what he had accomplished in such a short time.

But his response came fast, almost reflexive.

"Don't congratulate me. I'm not there yet."

That's the gap talking.

Robert had achieved what so many aspire to, but his inner narrative hadn't caught up. His old identity, the one shaped by years of corporate conditioning, was still grappling with the idea that this success could be his. That he could stand fully in it without waiting for the other shoe to drop.

The Tyranny of "Not Enoughness"

Robert, like so many of my clients, struggled with what one of them once called "not enoughness." No matter what he achieved, it never felt like enough. Every win was just a stepping stone to the next goal, and every milestone felt small compared to the bigger dreams still out of reach. He was constantly measuring himself against everything he hadn't done yet.

This mindset of always looking ahead was a double-edged sword. On one hand, it fueled his ambition, pushing him to accomplish more. On the other, it kept him in a constant state of dissatisfaction. He was stuck in the gap between where he was and where he thought he should be.

This is more than a mindset thing—it's hardwired into our brains. Remember the hedonic treadmill from Chapter Two? It's the idea that no matter how much we achieve, we quickly adapt and start chasing the next high. That's dopamine at work.

Dopamine gets called the "feel-good hormone," but it's really about motivation. It's what makes us crave more—more knowledge, more challenge, more adventure. It's why you feel a little thrill when your phone dings with a new message. It's the same drive that pushes someone to climb

Mount Everest or dive deep into the mysteries of black holes.

It's what keeps us moving forward. But when left unchecked, it can also keep us feeling like we're never quite there.

Steven Kotler better explains the role of dopamine in goal setting in his book *Art of the Impossible*.

It's released not just when we achieve a goal but also when we set one due to our brain's function to link cause and effect. When we have a history of setting and achieving goals, our brain links the goal setting with a reward, even before the reward is attained.

In the late 1990s, for example, Cambridge neuroscientist Wolfram Schultz gave monkeys a squirt of juice, which is a favorite monkey reward, and watched dopamine levels spike in their brains. At the beginning of the experiment, their brains released dopamine only when they got the actual juice. In time, this dopamine spike showed up earlier—for instance, when the lab door first opened. By the experiment's end, those spikes arose even earlier—when they heard footsteps in the hallway outside the laboratory's door.

Which means our brains are trained to reward the *pursuit*, not the pause. And when we don't consciously interrupt that loop? We internalize progress as something that only counts when it's "done," not when it's recognized. That's not ambition—that's neurochemistry on autopilot.

When Robert, like many others, kept chasing the next big goal without pausing to appreciate how far he'd come, he was stuck in a dopamine loop—always wanting, never truly having. It's like being on a treadmill that never stops. No matter how much you accomplish, the finish line keeps moving.

The problem? This constant state of striving can quietly fuel self-doubt and a sense of scarcity. And if it goes unchecked, it can take a real toll, leading to anxiety, burnout, and even depression. Because when nothing ever feels like enough, how can you ever feel at peace?

The Fear and Power of Acknowledgment

"Celebrate your wins" gets thrown around like easy-to-implement wisdom, but why are high achievers like yourself so reluctant to embrace it?

For many high achievers, especially those of us who have had to work twice as hard to be seen, heard, and valued, pausing to acknowledge success can feel...uncomfortable. Maybe even risky.

There's often this quiet, persistent fear: *If I slow down, will I lose my momentum? If I take a moment to celebrate, will I stop being seen as serious, capable, or hungry?*

This hesitation doesn't come from nowhere. It's shaped by the systems we've had to navigate, the messages we've internalized, and the double standards we've been measured against.

Here's what often fuels it:

- **Fear of Complacency:** Many of us have been conditioned to believe that constant striving is the only way to stay ahead—that if we pause, even for a moment, we risk falling behind in systems that weren't built for us to succeed in the first place.

- **Societal Expectations:** We live in a culture that glorifies *busyness*, that ties our worth to productivity. For many high achievers, especially those at the margins, this pressure to do more and be more is relentless—and pausing feels like breaking the rules.

- **Fear of Judgment:** For women of color and others navigating dominant cultures, celebrating wins can feel like opening the door to accusations of arrogance or self-promotion—as if pride in our accomplishments makes us "too much."

- **Belief in Endless Improvement:** There's always another level, another hurdle, another milestone. So instead of letting ourselves feel the joy of what we've accomplished, we focus on what's still missing—because that's what we've been taught will keep us safe.

Why This Mindset Backfires

"The horizon is an invaluable directional tool, but it's a disastrous measurement tool."—Dan Sullivan, *The Gap and the Gain*

When you're stuck in that "not there yet" mindset, it doesn't just mess with your self-perception—it silently hijacks your behavior. You become addicted to motion. Addicted to proving. Addicted to *doing*.

And not necessarily the kind of doing that moves the needle, but the kind that keeps you busy enough to avoid the discomfort of celebrating how far you've come.

Here's what that looks like in practice:

- You say yes to another project instead of pausing to acknowledge the one you just crushed.

- You tweak that deck, again, instead of sending it with confidence.

- You scroll LinkedIn looking for what others are doing, only to convince yourself you're not doing enough.

- You make plans to rest...after your next win. And then the next one.

That kind of busyness is not ambition. It's avoidance dressed up in productivity.

But that's not the only cost. This mindset also creates a PR problem, and for high-achieving women and women of color, that's the quiet killer of visibility and advancement.

You're doing excellent work—work that's often transformational. But because you don't feel "there yet," you downplay it. You bury it. You move on too quickly.

Meanwhile, someone with half your credentials, a quarter of your results, and 100% more audacity is already polishing up their LinkedIn post or pitching themselves as a thought leader.

They're in the spotlight—not because they're more qualified, but because they're louder, bolder, and less burdened by the "work twice as hard" tax.

This is how brilliant women get overlooked. It's not always about competence, but about visibility. And if you're constantly skipping your own celebration, brushing off your achievements, or waiting until the next annual performance review or until you're *really* "there" before you speak up? You're not being modest or humble. You're unintentionally making yourself invisible.

Let's be blunt:

- The reward for staying humble and quiet is being forgotten.

- The cost of never feeling "enough" is staying behind while others pass you by.

- The trade-off of grinding without reflection is success without recognition, and burnout without a break.

It's time to interrupt that cycle.

The Celebration Gap (a.k.a. Tom Cruise Science)

Let's start with the science (and not the Scientology kind):

Research out of Rutgers University found that recalling your past wins triggers a legit chemical reaction in your brain. When you reflect on what you've accomplished, your brain releases endorphins and serotonin, a.k.a. the feel-good squad that boosts your well-being and takes the edge off dopamine's constant demand for more, better, faster.

In short: remembering your wins changes your brain.

Okaaaaay, so what does any of this have to do with Tom Cruise?

I know the word "patience" goes down like dog food to a high achiever such as yourself, but I'm getting there!

Picture the last action movie you watched—maybe *Mission: Impossible*, *The Bourne Identity*, or some other film where the lead character runs across a rooftop like gravity is optional.

There's always *that* moment:

The hero (let's say Tom Cruise, because of course) has been leaping confidently from rooftop to rooftop. They're easy jumps to him, some might even say familiar territory.

Then *boom*, he hits **the big gap**.

It's wider, riskier, and more dangerous than any he's come across before.

He stops right at the edge, chest heaving, eyes locked on the distance. Because jumping from where he's standing? That's a free fall.

So what does he do?

He doesn't leap blindly. He backs up.

Now picture this: as Tom Cruise walks backward across that rooftop, he's creating space while scanning his mental highlight reel. Remembering the jumps he *has* made. The stunts he's survived. The literal and metaphorical explosions he's walked away from in slow motion.

He's gathering evidence:

I've done hard things before. I've landed leaps that scared the hell out of me. I've trained for this.

Then he runs.

And he clears the biggest gap yet.

That's what celebrating your past wins does. It's not just cute advice from your therapist or coach. It's a tactical, neurological reset that fuels you for the next leap.

It keeps your brain from staying stuck in survival mode, always panicking about what's next. And most importantly? It reminds you that you've done the impossible before. So even if you're not "there yet," you've got enough to keep going.

Take the Three-by-Three Challenge

When my high-achieving clients struggle with confidence as they push toward their next level, I give them a simple but powerful exercise: the Three-by-Three Challenge.

For three weeks, I challenge them to dedicate a few minutes at the end of their workday to document three wins they experienced that day (they can exceed this number if they want). Then follow it up with three (and no, they are not allowed to exceed three) priorities that they will tackle the next day by answering the question *"What three things will I need to complete tomorrow in order to feel accomplished?"*

That's it. Just a few minutes of reflection.

But the impact? Huge.

Instead of ending the day feeling behind, overwhelmed, or stuck in a loop of "I didn't do enough," because they've defined what "enough" is, they start recognizing their progress. They see the challenges they've overcome, which fuels their confidence and momentum.

By the end of the first week, many report tackling new challenges with more resilience and optimism. Less procrastination. More progress. A mindset shift that accelerates their growth without adding more to their plate.

It's proof that success isn't just about pushing forward—it's also about taking a moment to acknowledge how far you've already come.

Putting It into Practice: The Three-by-Three Challenge

Try it today. Take five quiet minutes right now to complete this exercise. You'll close your day with clarity, momentum, and confidence—not just a running to-do list.

Part One: Name three wins

What went well today? These don't have to be huge wins. Maybe you had a tough conversation. Maybe you made progress on a task that's been lingering. Maybe you simply showed up for yourself in a way that matters (including reading this book today).

Today's wins:

1.

2.

3.

Part Two: Set three priorities for tomorrow

What are the three things that, if you accomplish them, will allow you to feel satisfied and successful tomorrow? No more than three—clarity is power.

Tomorrow's priorities:

1.

2.

3.

Bonus action: Try this reflection activity for the rest of the week. Then another week. And then another. Because the next time you stand at the edge of a bigger leap, you won't be guessing—you'll be running toward it with receipts in hand.

Receipts

You've made a powerful shift in this chapter, and whether it felt subtle or seismic, it matters. Here's what you've just done:

- You named the invisible pressure that high achievers carry to always be producing and rarely be seen.

- You identified how dopamine-driven striving can trap even the most accomplished people in a loop of "not enough."

- You understood that acknowledging your wins is not weakness—it's a *strategic neurological advantage*.

- You exposed the invisibility tax so many brilliant women and professionals of color pay when they downplay their progress.

- You challenged the false belief that rest equals regression—and celebration means complacency.

- You reframed celebration not as a luxury, but as a discipline of visibility, clarity, and fuel.

- You were introduced to a tool—the Three-by-Three Challenge—that can shift your mindset from scarcity to sufficiency, one day at a time.

The old version of you might have pushed through this chapter without pause, already chasing the next insight.

But here you are. You stopped. You reflected. You celebrated.

And that? That's real progress.

Your Next Move

You've begun to see the gap for what it is—a sign that you're evolving, not failing. You're also noticing the stories that fill that gap. The ones that whisper you're behind, you're not enough, or you don't belong here.

This week, pause and listen. When those stories arise, don't rush past them or drown them out with more striving.

And then, ask yourself: If I were in the room, truly claiming my space, my voice, my right to belong, what new story would I choose instead?

That's where we're headed next: rewriting those narratives so that your inner dialogue helps you stay in the room, not shrink within it.

Change your story. Change your life.

#BeInTheRoom

Chapter Seven

The Story I'm Telling Myself Is... – Rewriting Your Inner Authority

By now, we've explored how invisible ropes, limiting beliefs, and the tyranny of *not enough* shape the way we move through the world. We've practiced naming our fears, choosing our hard, partnering with our self-doubt, and reflecting on our wins.

But the truth about all that work is that it isn't just about changing your thoughts. It's about changing the stories that have shaped your identity.

Because identity—that's the deepest narrative of all. It's the story we don't even realize we're telling ourselves—the one that defines what we believe we deserve, how we show up, and whether we give ourselves permission to claim space in the first place.

And I know this because I've lived it.

I am not here to prove my worth. I am here to do the work.

Choosing Identity Over Insecurity

Let's revisit a moment I shared with you earlier—when I walked into that room of senior executives alongside my co-facilitator, Glen.

You know how it started: The slow, shaky breath. The sound of my heels echoing louder than felt comfortable. The weight of their gaze—or what I thought was their gaze—pulling my shoulders down.

But what I didn't share in Chapter One is what happened next.

In that moment of spiraling doubt, I remembered everything I've written about in these pages so far. I caught myself in the act of telling an old, familiar story:

They don't think I belong.

I need my bio to prove I'm worthy.

If I fuck this up, it will confirm every bias they've ever held about women like me.

But this time? I had tools.

I named the fear. (Chapter Four: Too Many F-Words)

I challenged the voice. (Chapter Five: Stop Calling It Impostor Syndrome)

I looked for the gap between my perception and reality. (Chapter Six: Don't Hold Your Applause)

And as Glen skipped the bios and the room turned to me, I made a decision:

I practiced being the person I wanted to be.

I stood tall, even if my heart raced. I spoke clearly (I mean, for the most part. There were still some nervous stammers and filler words), even if my inner critic whispered doubts.

I reminded myself: *I am not here to prove my worth. I am here to do the work.*

It wasn't about faking confidence. It was about choosing a new story in real time—one action, one word, one breath at a time.

And that's how it starts.

The Power of a False Narrative

The stories I tell myself are often all-consuming and, frankly, debilitating.

When I look back on the situation above and countless others like it, I realize I had no proof of the story in my head. I had no proof that these people thought I was underqualified or that they automatically assumed my inferiority.

My reaction was a response to a story I told myself.

I am fortunate enough to say that all my career, I've been surrounded by mentors and sponsors who rooted for my success. And you may find this surprising, but they have been predominantly white men.

But my personal history doesn't override the realities of being a Black woman in corporate America or negate the discrimination against many others. It just doesn't excuse the assumptions I acted upon.

And this was just one of the stories I told myself.

I have countless others my brain sewed together, which influence how I move in the world, handle situations, and approach people. And it's not just me. It's my clients, from CEOs and entrepreneurs to tutors and students, who all have their own stories weighing them down.

We have these stories we tell ourselves that we believe are real and keep us limited. They keep us held back and contained.

And here's what I've learned: These stories shape not only what we think, but they shape who we become.

Standing in that room with the eyes of those executives on me, I wasn't just having insecure thoughts. I was fighting an identity I'd carried for years.

The identity of the "outsider." The background player who wrote the scripts so that others could shine. The one who has to work twice as hard. The one who can't afford to stumble because people like her don't get a second chance. The one who does things perfectly or not at all.

This wasn't about a missing bio. It was about a missing belief in myself.

We don't just tell stories; we become them. And when we don't question the script, we keep playing the same role.

But identity, like story, can be rewritten.

Deciding Who's Running the Show

Think of your identity as the CEO of your decision making. She's the one calling the shots, whether you realize it or not.

Let me ask you a question:

Ever work for a CEO or a boss whose decisions made zero sense to you? No vision. No transparency. No logic.

They'd show up late to the meeting with a shiny new "strategy," dump it on your desk, and expect miracles by Monday.

You sat there thinking:

If I were in charge, I'd run this place completely different.

The great thing about that CEO is that we know exactly what their mission is and what they stand for. I mean, it's on the damn website and they repeat it ad nauseum every mandatory town hall meeting.

What if there was a CEO running the company from behind the scenes? You didn't know their face. They never spoke clearly to their mandate or gave any rationale to support their decisions. They just moved in silence and, often, a quiet sabotage.

Sounds toxic as hell, right?

Now here's the plot twist: That invisible CEO? She might be running *your* company. *Your* life.

Because every single one of us has an internal operating system—a belief system quietly driving decisions behind the scenes. Most of us never stop to audit it.

We don't ask:

- Who wrote these rules I'm living by?

- Why do I keep defaulting to safety, silence, or perfection?

- What voice is actually running this show?

Let me put it like this: If your life were a company, **who's been sitting in the CEO chair of your mind?**

Who's been deciding what's possible for you?

What rooms you walk into?

What chances you take—or don't?

For years, my CEO was the cautious version of myself: brilliant at minimizing risk, keeping me safe, and ensuring I stayed in good standing.

Her go-to phrases were:

- "Let's wait until we're more ready."

- "Don't rock the boat."

- "Make sure everyone else is okay with it first."

- "If you do this, you're taking away the opportunity from someone who might deserve it more."

And that served me for a while. But eventually, I realized she was holding me back. Every bold move felt like a boardroom battle. Every opportunity got a "maybe later" stamp.

So I fired her.

Not with anger, but with gratitude for getting me this far.

She was a great starter CEO. But she wasn't built to run a company with this kind of vision, scale, or impact.

I promoted a new one—the version of me that:

- Believes in bold strategy and soul-aligned action.

- Knows that fear is data, not a directive.

- Leads from purpose, not perfection.

- Makes moves now—not once the website is perfect and everyone approves.

You Can't Build a Legacy if You're Still Reporting to a Ghost

If you don't consciously choose who runs your internal company, you will default to the most over-practiced voice in your head.

And often, it's not even yours.

It's the voice of:

- The parent who taught you success = safety.

- The teacher who said you're "too much."

- The boss who praised your silence over your strategy.

- The culture that convinced you ambition should be quiet.

And if you let *that* CEO stay in power?

- You'll build a life full of gold stars and quiet resentment.

- You'll watch less-qualified people take the stage while you rewrite your email draft for the fifth time.

- You'll wonder why your life looks successful—but doesn't feel like it.

The risk isn't failure. **The risk is success on someone else's terms.**

Now it's your turn: Who has been the CEO of your decisions? Is it the cautious protector? The perfectionist? The voice of someone else's expectations? And who do you want at the helm moving forward?

Putting It into Practice: Fire and Hire Your Inner CEO

It's time to conduct a performance review. Use this space to reflect and write down your responses.

Identify your current CEO.

Who has been making the final call in your internal boardroom? What story do they tell to justify their decisions? How has this CEO protected you? How have they limited you?

Thank and release them

What has this CEO helped you survive or accomplish? Why is it time for a leadership change?

Hire your new CEO

Describe your new CEO. What are their values? How do they make decisions? How do they see your worth, your potential, your future?

First act of business

Identify one decision you will make this week as if your new CEO is in charge.

Commit to it.

Receipts

By the end of this chapter, here's what you've done:

- **Named the hidden script behind your thoughts.**

- You identified that the stories driving your decisions aren't just passing ideas—they're deeply ingrained narratives that shape your identity, actions, and outcomes.

- **Recognized that your internal voice isn't always your own.**

  - You paused to reflect on whose voice has been making the decisions. Was it a protective version of you? A cultural expectation? An old authority figure? You started to separate your truth from inherited beliefs.

- **Understood that identity is not fixed—it's chosen.**

  - You learned that your internal CEO can be replaced. You are allowed to let go of the one who led with fear, perfectionism, or people pleasing—and promote someone who leads with vision, courage, and alignment.

- **Practiced shifting from reaction to intention.**

  - You didn't just analyze your self-talk—you took real steps to rewrite the story in real time. Whether in a boardroom or in front of your mirror, you practiced becoming who you want to be before you're fully comfortable there.

- **Took back the pen.**

  - You stopped letting outdated stories write the next chapter of your life. You chose a new narrative—and with it, a new standard for how you show up, make decisions, and lead yourself.

Your Next Steps

Let's take a moment to acknowledge just how far you've come.

At the start of this book, we made a commitment—to name the invisible weight you've been carrying, to challenge the internalized scripts that have shaped your sense of worth, and to start leading from a place of alignment, not exhaustion.

In **Part One**, you did the courageous work of slowing down to see the hidden toll of success. You faced the quiet tension that most high achievers avoid, and you gave yourself permission to say, *"I'm carrying too much."*

In **Part Two**, you dismantled the stories that kept you in survival mode. You named the real culprits behind self-doubt and impostor syndrome. You stopped pathologizing your ambition and started reclaiming the mic from voices that never belonged in your internal boardroom in the first place.

Each chapter brought you closer to the core aim of this book:

To help you stop contorting yourself to fit rooms that were never designed for your brilliance—and to start shaping the ones where you belong.

And now, you're ready.

In **Part Three**, we go from internal to external. From mindset to moves.

This is where you stop asking, *"Who am I to lead?"* and start answering, *"Who do I want to become as I lead?"*

You'll explore what it looks like to show up fully in your vision—not just thinking differently, but choosing differently. Because rewriting the story is powerful. But **living into a new identity?** That's legacy work.

Let's begin.

It's time to stop waiting for permission. It's time to stop just surviving the rooms you enter—and start leading in them. It's time to design a life that doesn't just feel like enough, but feels like yours.

Part Three
That Thing You Keep Calling Crazy? It's Actually Clarity

CLAIMING THE VISION

Purpose isn't found. It's built. Clarity in motion

#BeInTheRoom

Chapter Eight

Purpose, Passions, and Strengths, Oh My! – How to Build Your Internal Compass

In the last chapter, you took the bold step of re-evaluating who's running the show—your inner CEO. Now it's time to ask: Where is she taking you? What's guiding her choices, her risks, her next moves? That's where your internal compass comes in.

And I'm going to be real with you, this is the part of the book where things start to get a little squishy. Words like *purpose* and *calling* get tossed around like confetti at a New Age retreat, and somehow you're expected to know exactly what you're here on earth to do...or else.

It's almost laughable how mystical this conversation gets. Like in order to "find your purpose," you have to quit your job, move to Bali, and lick the back of a toad under a full moon in Pisces. Or, if you're lucky, maybe you stumble upon it while journaling with crystals. Either way, the message is clear: purpose is for the chosen few who are willing to go on an existential scavenger hunt.

I was reminded of this while watching one of the *Superman* movies—not because I'm a comic book nerd (please, this is as far as my superhero knowledge goes), but because of how *clear* Superman's purpose was. This man literally arrived on earth with a voice memo from his dead planet telling him who he was, what he was meant to do, and why his powers existed.

Like, excuse me?

He didn't have to figure it out through therapy or spiral into an identity crisis every time his LinkedIn headline didn't feel "aligned." No, he had a literal intergalactic *mission statement.* Protect the humans. Use your powers for good. Boom. Done.

And the rest of us? We're out here cracking open fortune cookies hoping one of them finally hits.

This is the trap so many of us fall into. We believe that purpose should come to us like a divine telegram. That some higher power is going to slide a sealed envelope across the table one day with our "why" written in calligraphy. So we wait. And we wander. And in the meantime, we let other people plot the course.

Because here's what happens when you don't wire your own internal GPS: **someone else does it for you.**

Society will hand you a preloaded destination: Success = title, salary, corner office.

Your family might have expectations baked in: Be stable, practical, and don't take risks.

Your company certainly has a route planned: Stay in your lane. Hit your KPIs. Wait your turn.

And before you know it, you're years down a road you never actually chose, wondering how the hell you got here, and why it doesn't feel right.

The real danger isn't that you'll fail to find your purpose.

It's that you'll forget you even get to define it.

When we don't pause to build an internal compass—to ask what matters, what lights us up, what strengths we want to bring forward—we default to chasing whatever external metric is screaming the loudest.

And then one day you look up and realize...

You're living a life that looks good on paper, but doesn't *feel* good in your soul.

You're successful, but not fulfilled.

You're moving fast, but you're not going anywhere that matters.

So no, your purpose isn't going to show up in a sky-written message or at the bottom of your overpriced matcha latte. (Unpopular opinion? I don't even like matcha. Or lattes.)

It's built, not found. Calibrated over time. And it starts with tuning out the noise and tuning into you.

Purpose vs. Passion

Many people struggle with the idea that purpose and paying the bills can coexist. This limiting belief brings us back to the concepts we explored in Chapter One: the invisible ropes, the stories we internalize, and the idea that work must either be a grind for survival or an unattainable altruistic dream. But the truth? Purpose doesn't always have to come from your job, and it doesn't have to look like launching a charity.

And I can hear you already: *"But Lauren, I don't know what I'm passionate about!"*

Here's the good news: You don't need to know.

We often confuse purpose with passion, as if they are one and the same. But let me be honest: I'm not sure I even know what passion truly means anymore. Passion can feel fleeting—like a hobby that brings joy without necessarily fulfilling a deeper calling. I might be passionate about cooking, but that doesn't mean I want to make a career out of it. And sometimes, the pressure of tying your livelihood to your passion can dim the very joy that passion brings.

Here's what I've learned and what I see time and again with my clients: a fulfilling career is built on three essential pillars. (Spoiler alert: None of which are passion.)

First, leveraging your strengths: doing work that taps into your natural talents and allows you to excel with confidence.

Second, fulfilling your purpose: contributing to something bigger than yourself, creating meaning that resonates with who you are.

Third, aligning with your values: working in ways and environments that reflect what matters most to you at your core.

When these three elements come together, that's when work starts to feel not just successful, but truly fulfilling.

Many of my clients come to me because the rooms they're in don't leverage their strengths—or their work no longer aligns with their deeper purpose or values. And when that happens, the disconnection is palpable.

I think of a client, a Black female lawyer, who shared her struggle with me during one of our sessions.

"They want me to become a judge," she said, sighing over video call.

"Who does?" I asked.

"Everyone. My boss, my mentors, my colleagues. They want to put my name forth for a judge opening."

To anyone else, this might seem like a positive opportunity, and my initial reaction was the same. But I sensed something deeper at play.

"And you don't want that?" I probed.

She looked ashamed as she replied, *"No. They're pushing me to be a judge because they need more representation of Black women on the bench, but I don't feel like it's right for me."*

We had previously discussed her desire to best leverage her strengths and interests, which lay more in advocacy than in the judicial system. Yet, as a minority, she felt pressure to fill a visible role that wasn't true to her purpose.

Through our sessions, we explored her strengths and passions, uncovering her interest in Indigenous cultures, rooted in her mother's work as a nurse who flew into Indigenous reserves. This personal connection ignited her passion for education and awareness regarding information privilege.

She began seeking opportunities to speak out on that platform instead of following the path others envisioned for her. However, stepping away from the expectations of other Black female lawyers felt scary to her—as it does for many whose calling is different from an obvious path of representative trailblazing.

For me, the fear of leaving my corporate job was rooted in the idea that my absence could mean one less woman of color in leadership. I wondered if it would be selfish to pursue my own path at the cost of representation. But then I realized that by removing myself from that position, I could create a broader impact elsewhere while opening the door for someone else to fill the position whose interests and purpose aligned with this field.

I came to see that we each serve best where we are most fulfilled; where our strengths, purpose, and values align.

And here's the most important part: You don't need to make a grand impact to validate your choices. Your life doesn't need to be a TED Talk or a headline-worthy act of service. Sharing your wisdom with a mentee, showing up for your team with integrity, modeling courage in your community— this is impact too.

When we stop chasing someone else's definition of purpose or impact, and start living our own, that's when our work starts to truly matter.

Your Day Job Is Your Training Ground

Maybe you're reading this and thinking, *Cool, Lauren. But what if I'm still in the wrong role? What if I don't have the luxury of aligning my values, strengths, and purpose yet?*

Good. Stay with me.

Because here's the secret I wish more people said out loud: **Your current job might be the best-paid training program you'll ever have.**

I know it might feel like the furthest thing from your purpose. But resentment burns energy—energy you'll need for your next chapter.

Instead of stewing, start studying. That's exactly what I did in corporate as I was thinking of my next move.

- I coached colleagues and mentees on the clock.

- Facilitated strategy retreats.

- Led our Black Professionals ERG.

- Launched an internal podcast.

I made my nine-to-five my lab. Every skill I sharpened on their dime paid off when I launched my business.

So ask yourself:

- What systems here would I steal for my own business?

- What leadership mistakes do I never want to repeat?

- What opportunities can I raise my hand for to sharpen my voice and build my confidence?

Take notes. Shadow leaders. Practice in meetings you'd normally shrink in. Because purpose doesn't mean you have to *love* every second (I'm living my purpose, and to be honest, I *love* it maybe 60% of the time). It means finding meaning and new ways to leverage your strengths while you *build what's next*.

Discovering Your Strengths

Sometimes, your strengths don't feel like strengths right away. You're nervous, shaking in your heels, sweating profusely, or maybe all three at once. That was me, at least.

One of the first times I realized speaking to others was one of my strengths was when I was asked to speak for a national event at my corporate job. It was for a Women Leaders Who Inspire talk, and I remember the overwhelming terror I felt. I was convinced I was going to bomb it—big time. My palms were clammy, and my heart felt like it was about to leap out of my chest. But still, I stood up there and did the talk.

When I walked off the stage, expecting to collapse from sheer relief, something unexpected happened. People approached me from all directions. And then the most meaningful compliment of all came from a woman who said, "Oh my gosh, I didn't know it was possible for us. I didn't know we could be directors. You changed my perspective. You captured how I felt when I thought I was alone in it."

My eyebrows were in my hairline at that point.

Me? I made people feel that way?

I was just speaking my truth, sharing what was real for me. And yet it resonated so deeply with others. That day changed how I saw myself. I remember leaving the event on an incredible high, not just because I'd survived it but because I had actually made a difference.

But the catch was, I hadn't felt strong at all while doing it. If anything, I felt vulnerable and exposed. I realized that sometimes, your greatest strengths might not come wrapped in confidence. They might come wrapped in nerves, in fear. But that doesn't mean they aren't strengths.

In retrospect, I can see how my path was being built long before I realized it. The seemingly insignificant moments and decisions were quietly laying the foundation. I didn't notice at the time, but I was paving the way for my future. And looking back, I realize that many of us have already been building our paths, even when it feels like we're stuck.

We just don't give ourselves enough credit.

So many times, I thought the place I wanted to be—anywhere but my corporate job—was so far away. It felt impossible, like a distant dream I couldn't reach. But what I discovered was that I needed to zoom in.

Chances are, you've been doing work to get yourself a little closer to your dream, too. You're probably already halfway there, but you don't even realize it. We're all so hard on ourselves that we fail to see the progress we've made. We focus on the wall we have yet to climb and overlook the bricks we've already laid.

The bricks are your experiences. They're your strengths. They're the opportunities you've created or seized along the way. Each one of those bricks shrinks the gap between you and the goals that once felt unattainable.

Back in my corporate days, we had this ritual every January where the directors would get our annual revenue targets. Without fail, once the numbers were revealed, we'd all look at each other and say, *"There's no fuckin' way!"* The targets were always higher than the previous year, even though we hadn't hit those targets either. It felt like we were being set up to fail. We couldn't see the way forward because we were focused on the size of the wall.

But despite all our protests, one fact remained: the target was the target, and it wasn't going to change.

What did change, however, was how we approached it. In 2019, we exceeded our plan for the first time in decades, and it wasn't because the target was suddenly achievable—it was because we took a different approach. We gathered all our bricks and became laser-focused on how to close the gap.

Instead of fixating on the whole $10 million wall, we broke it down. First, we identified the bricks we already had—$3 million worth of revenue from projects already sold. Those bricks were laid, and the wall began to take shape. Next, we focused on high-probability revenue—the bricks we could see but hadn't quite cemented yet. That added another $2 million. Now, instead of a $10 million goal, we were left with a $5 million gap to fill.

Every week, we met to come up with new ideas, to move opportunities from low probability to high, and to lay more bricks. Week by week, the wall grew. Not only did this process boost our creativity and accountability, but it also shifted our mindset. We were no longer overwhelmed by the enormity of the goal. We were focused on the specific, actionable steps we could take to shrink the gap.

For the first time, we exceeded our targets. But more importantly, we learned how to assess where we were, recognize what strengths and opportunities we already had, and focus on where we needed support.

This is exactly what you need to do when assessing your own strengths. You have to play into them, and you have to find the moments when you feel most in your skin. For me, one of those moments was public speaking. But even though people would tell me, "You're really good at this," I didn't believe it right away. It took personal reflection and inventory to see what others saw.

That's when I started asking myself: What parts of these experiences do I love? What makes me feel confident? I realized I loved being on stage, telling a story, connecting with people, and inspiring them. I may not have had the full picture yet, but I knew I needed more of those moments.

The key to finding your strengths lies in those moments when you feel aligned, when you feel a spark. Once you identify them, you can start to build from there, piece by piece, brick by brick.

Revealing Hidden Strengths

Knowing your strengths isn't easy. A lot of clients come to me, and they don't know what to do next. That's literally the point of my job.

I could share a dozen stories like this, but one that always stands out is Amanda.

During one of our sessions, Amanda sat across from me, insisting she was "not good at anything."

I fought to keep a straight face. Amanda was a professional singer who'd taken a break to explore different career paths.

Somehow, in those months away, she'd lost sight of what she was capable of.

"Didn't you land a contract with Universal Records to sing?" I asked.

She sighed, looking exasperated. *"Yeah, but that was years ago."*

I leaned in a little. *"Your strengths don't just disappear because you took a break, Amanda. You're a singer. You have a powerful voice."*

"But I don't feel called to sing anymore," she said, almost as if admitting defeat.

Her words hung in the air for a moment, and I could tell how much they weighed on her. It's a feeling I've seen many times before. Sometimes, the most obvious use of our strengths doesn't feel aligned with our purpose anymore. But that doesn't mean our strengths are gone, or that we can't use them in ways we never considered.

"Your voice isn't limited to singing," I said finally.

She blinked, looking up. I could see the wheels turning in her mind. Amanda had been so focused on the things people told her she wasn't good at, she'd lost sight of her most natural gift—her voice.

"How else can you use your voice?" I asked, giving her space to explore.

She thought about it, her mouth twisting to one side. *"I guess I could do podcasts. Maybe use it to advocate for others?"*

"Exactly."

At that moment, Amanda realized her voice wasn't confined to just one path. She could tell stories, inspire people, and champion causes she cared about. Her voice was her strength. It had just been waiting for her to rediscover it.

What we did next was to pull that strength forward. Amanda began to see that her next move didn't have to look like the last one. She could center her voice—her greatest asset—in a way that truly aligned with her values and goals. Once she acknowledged her strength, new opportunities started revealing themselves.

Purpose Alignment, Black Excellence, and Bias

Sometimes our strengths are overshadowed by bias, whether it's the biases of others or our own.

I want to share two stories that highlight just how deeply ingrained my own biases were. When I first moved to L.A., my sister and I attended an event—a normal occurrence in her world. We entered a beautiful and extravagant house, complete with three luxury cars parked outside. As we approached, my curiosity overwhelmed me: *Who lived here? What kind of job did they have to afford this lifestyle?*

To my (shameful) surprise, the owner was a Black man around my age. At that moment, my biases surfaced. I couldn't comprehend how he'd achieved such success. And, ironically, he wore a hat that boldly proclaimed, *Black Excellence.*

This moment struck me. There's an automatic association we have: When we see a white person achieving certain levels of success, we think, *Oh, that makes sense.* But when we see a Black person, we question, *What happened here?* I recognized that this bias lived within me, influencing how I viewed success.

When I launched my business, I found myself hesitating to target people of color, fearing that they wouldn't have the income to afford my services. I questioned whether I would sign up for charity work. It's a wild bias to hold. Society teaches us that Black excellence is rare, reinforcing the idea that those striving for it are on a solitary path.

But I thought back to the women of color who approached me after the Women Leaders Who Inspire talk and realized I not only had a strength in speaking to this audience, but needed to continue to do so.

I wanted to surround myself with more examples of Black excellence to combat the biases forming (and already formed) in my mind and, perhaps most importantly, those my children were beginning to internalize as well. It pains me to acknowledge that not only did I struggle with these biases, but my children were starting to form them, too.

One evening, before we moved to L.A., my family sat around the dinner table discussing our dreams. My son spoke up, saying, *"I want to make a difference."* I smiled; so many children share that aspiration.

"How would you like to do that?" I asked.

He picked at his corn and replied, *"I think advocating, doing presentations, and speeches are good ways, but I need a partner."*

"Why would you need a partner?" I probed.

"I need to partner with a white person so that I have credibility."

My heart sank. My husband and I exchanged a concerned glance. My son had internalized the myth of not even Black excellence, but Black credibility, reflecting my own biases back at me.

It was crucial for me to break this cycle. I wanted to create an environment where my children could see Black excellence and credibility as the norm, rather than the exception. Now, we live in a neighborhood rich with diversity—beautiful homes, successful Black families. I no longer question it, and neither does my son.

That moment lit a fire. This is my purpose, and I choose it daily.

Put It into Practice: Mapping Your Three Pillars

Use this space to reflect and capture insights as you start aligning your career (or broader life choices) with your strengths, purpose, and values. Return to earlier notes and exercises (such as your wins from the Three-by-Three Challenge or your Strengths reflection) to guide you.

Strengths

Look back on moments when you felt energized, confident, or proud of what you contributed. What natural abilities or skills were you using? What comes easily to you that others recognize and appreciate? Examples might include: facilitating, problem solving, advocating, mentoring, designing, analyzing, or storytelling.

Tip: You might want to revisit the "ing" words you wrote down in the Practice section of Chapter Two.

What are three to five core strengths you want to bring into your work and life more intentionally?

Purpose

What are the moments in your current or past roles when you felt most lit up? What were you doing? Who were you serving? Examples might include: empowering others, advancing equity, creating beauty, solving complex problems, and building community.

Values

Consider the principles that matter most in how you work and live. What do you need in your environment to thrive? What do you want your work to reflect? Examples might include: integrity, creativity, freedom, collaboration, learning, and service.

What are three to five values that you want to center as you move forward?

Reflection

Looking at what you've written: Where do you see alignment between your strengths, purpose, and values? Where do you see gaps? What small steps could you take to bring these three pillars into closer alignment in your work or life?

Remember: This is a living document. Your purpose, strengths, and values can evolve as you grow—and that's a good thing. The goal is not to have perfect clarity today, but to start aligning your daily actions with who you are and who you are becoming.

Receipts

Let's recap what you've just done:

- You untangled the myths around purpose, passion, and calling—and gave yourself permission to build, not find, your purpose.

- You identified the **three pillars** that guide a fulfilling career: your strengths, your purpose, and your values.

- You began shifting the narrative from *"I don't know what I'm good at"* to *"I've already been building this path brick by brick."*

- You reframed your current role—from a drain on your purpose to a paid training ground for your next chapter.

- You uncovered hidden strengths that may not come wrapped in confidence—but show up as impact, clarity, and deep resonance.

You're not waiting to feel aligned. You're *actively* aligning with who you are, what you stand for, and where you're going. And that clarity? That's what builds momentum.

Your Next Steps

Now that you've begun to map out your strengths, purpose, and values, it's time to think about what comes next.

Purpose is not just about what fulfills you—it's about what you leave behind. The mark you make. The space you create for others. The ripple effect of your choices, your courage, and your voice.

It's time to move from purpose to power. From intention to impact. From rewriting your story to building what comes after.

Staying small is selfish

#BeInTheRoom

Chapter Nine

It's Not About You, Boo – Your Legacy. Your Ambition. It's Bigger than You

Remember those intrinsic motivators—the ones that push you to leave a mark using your gifts, your knowledge, your growth? Now ask yourself: Who benefits from your stagnation? And who rises when you do?

How Your Growth Creates a Blueprint for Others

I recently read the book *Diary of a CEO* by Steven Bartlett, who expanded on the age-old principle of "filling your own bucket first." The idea here is in line with the "put your own oxygen mask on first" advice when on an airplane: You can't pour from an empty cup. Before we can help and uplift others, we need to be standing on solid ground ourselves. This is not just a matter of financial or material wealth, but also knowledge, skills, and emotional well-being.

Every time you learn something new, break down a barrier, or step into a bigger version of yourself, you're not just elevating yourself—you're also making space for others. The networks you build and the platforms you create all send a signal to the people around you: *This is possible*. Especially for those who have had fewer opportunities or haven't seen themselves represented before.

That's the start of legacy.

Because legacy is more than having your name on a building. It's about the ripple effect of your courage, the stories people tell after you leave the room, and the imprint you leave on others.

And the most powerful legacies often come from people who never intended to leave one. They were just doing what they felt called to do. The act of stepping fully into who you are, especially when it's uncomfortable, or when you've been told to stay small. Legacy isn't just about personal fulfillment. It becomes a blueprint for someone else.

I can relate to this firsthand. Leaving the security of my corporate job to chase a more purposeful path felt selfish. I wasn't used to being in the spotlight, and I constantly questioned whether I was taking up space meant for someone else. Thoughts like *Is my voice enough?* and *Who am I to think I can make a difference?* were loud and never ending.

That first year after I made the leap? Temptation called. I'd see LinkedIn alerts for chief of staff or IT operations roles and wonder if I should just go back. It would have been easier. But then I'd hear a voice in my head reminding me: *Lauren, this is bigger than you.*

From Personal Power to Collective Impact

Legacy thinking forces you to ask: *What would it look like to become the change I want to see—not just to wish it for others, but to embody it myself?*

Almost three years ago, I asked my kids what they wanted to be when they grew up. My nine-year-old daughter said she dreamed of being an interior designer on HGTV, but didn't think she could because "only white women get to do that." My eleven-year-old son wanted to be a YouTube star, but he believed he'd have to hide his Black identity at first to gain acceptance.

At first, that conversation broke me.

Then it became my fuel.

And here's the thing about legacy: It often begins as something you can't unsee. You come to the realization that your presence isn't just for you, and your decisions help write new scripts for the people watching. And that sometimes, the most radical thing you can do is step into your fullness because you know someone else needs the map.

And in my case, it was my children who helped me realize this.

Since then, I've helped hundreds of men and women, especially women of color, reach heights they once thought were impossible. I've seen them land higher-paying jobs in roles that align with their values, grow as leaders, and reclaim their time from burnout. I've watched them step into rooms with confidence, speak up for more representation, and push for equality, fairness, and justice.

Their transformations didn't start with external validation, but instead, they started with internal permission. Permission to say: *I want more.* To stop waiting for someone to hand them a blueprint and instead become the architect.

That's identity work.

And every step I take now ensures that one day, my kids—or theirs—will walk into any room without a second thought about whether they belong. They *will* belong.

So, if you've ever thought that the steps you need to take toward your own ambitions are selfish, remind yourself: staying small is the real selfishness. Because beneath all that noble-sounding sacrifice of "putting others first" is a quiet attempt to protect yourself from risk, visibility, and growth. Your ambition isn't just about you. It's about the people who will be inspired by your courage, the doors you'll open for others, and the change you'll create. Because when you rise, you lift others with you.

Still feeling guilty for wanting more?

Put It Into Practice: Map Your Legacy Ripple Effect

Reflect on your motivators

Who benefits from your growth, courage, or success? Consider your family, community, colleagues, or anyone who might see your journey as a blueprint.

What story do you want people to tell about you after you leave the room?

Think about how you want your presence, leadership, or contributions to be remembered.

What small act can you take this week to move toward that legacy?

Legacy isn't built in grand gestures—it starts with one courageous action at a time.

What old narrative or guilt might try to hold you back?

Write it down so you can recognize it for what it is.

What is your new permission statement?

Complete the sentence: I give myself permission to...

Receipts

Let's take a moment to acknowledge what you've just done in this chapter:

- You redefined legacy—not as what you leave behind when you're gone, but what you create through how you show up today.

- You gave yourself permission to want more—and started disentangling that desire from guilt.

- You began to recognize how your growth is a blueprint for others, especially those who haven't seen themselves represented.

- You identified how guilt, perfectionism, or over-functioning can mask fear and delay your impact.

- You reframed ambition—not as ego, but as a generous act of leadership and visibility.

- You looked beyond titles and outcomes to consider the ripple effect of your courage, voice, and decisions.

You've just taken a major step in claiming your power—not just for yourself, but for the people who will benefit because you chose not to shrink. That's legacy in motion.

Your Next Step

In this chapter, you didn't just reflect on legacy—you started building it. You mapped whom your growth impacts, what values you want to leave behind, and where guilt has been standing in your way. You began telling the truth about what your ambition really means—and who it's for.

As you move forward, hold this question with care and courage:

What is the room where your legacy will come alive, and what will it take to claim or create it?

That room might not exist yet. You might have to build it. But know this: you don't have to walk into it perfectly; you just have to walk in on purpose.

And if you're not sure what that next step looks like yet, don't worry.

We're going to build it—together.

I <u>do</u> know.
Dig deeper!

#BeInTheRoom

Chapter Ten

Stop Lying to Yourself (You Know What You Want) – From Fear-Based Reflexes to Fuck-It Energy

In leadership workshops I facilitate, I often encourage leaders to find strength in the vulnerability of admitting that they don't have the answers. But some of you take it way too far when it really counts.

Before we go any further, let me say something that might sting:

"I don't know" is rarely true. It's a reflex. A defense mechanism.

And if you've said it lately (or a thousand times), I want you to know you're not alone. You're human. But you're also readier than you think.

Just like Jeremy was when he sat across from me in a session and dropped his first *"I don't know."*

"I know that's not true." I shook my head and sighed. The man across from me was not only lying to me but to himself.

I knew he wasn't a malicious, intentional liar, but since the start of our session, he'd repeated the same lie in response to almost every question I asked.

"What do you want to do next?"

"I don't know."

"What would make you feel happy?"

"I don't know."

"Where do you want to be?"

"I. DON'T. KNOW!"

Jeremy, the vice president of sales at a medium-sized insurance company in the Midwest, sat across from me in the mustard-yellow chair. Most of my clients were virtual, but Jeremy was a longtime client who was in my neighborhood for the weekend, so I'd invited him to my home office.

He dug his thumbs into his eye sockets. *"I'm not lying,"* he insisted. *"I really don't know."*

I suppressed a small smile. When I'd first started coaching, responses similar to Jeremy's would result in frustration so powerful I'd want to rip my hair out. But I was used to it now. I expected to have to dig a little deeper to unlock my clients' true desires.

It was like there was a three-word script each of my clients instinctively knew to follow without ever talking to one another. This meant I wasn't surprised to hear Jeremy's uncertainty.

"I don't know" is a common defense mechanism. As a coach, I'm trained to see beyond this surface-level answer, understanding that it's often a cover for deeper, unarticulated desires.

"Sit with it. You do know." I paused a beat before continuing. *"There's no judgment here. I want to hear your most preposterous goals and dreams. No matter how big they are or how silly they seem, I promise you they aren't. Everyone's success starts with a dream."*

Jeremy squinted at me through his fingers. There it was, the validation he needed. We were close; he had an answer, but he wasn't quite ready to vocalize it yet.

I've come to learn that within every person I've worked with, there's a distinct voice at the point where the spine meets the skull—a voice that knows exactly what we desire and is itching to share. However, its message becomes muddled by layers of self-doubt and fear. Concerns like *Will this sound foolish?* or *What if vocalizing it commits me to this path?* lead to evasive replies like, *"It's not that simple"* and *"I don't know."*

I dug deeper, voicing this to Jeremy.

"There's a small voice in your head, isn't there? You know what you want. Or at least, it knows what it wants. Let me speak to that part of you."

It might sound silly, but I often ask my clients to let me speak directly to that little voice. It's a seemingly small request, but time and again, it unlocks their true desires, unfiltered by fear and amplified by curiosity and genuine longing.

That small voice is the voice of vision.

The Power of Visualization

But here's why this is harder than it sounds: Our brains don't naturally create futures that look wildly different from our past. Neuroscience tells us that our beliefs are formed from two types of memory, episodic (what we've experienced ourselves) and semantic (what we've observed in others). In other words, the limits of what we believe is possible are shaped by what we've seen or lived. Which is why it's so hard to imagine being in a different kind of room if you've never seen anyone like you in it.

That's why I incorporate visualization in my life and the lives of my clients. Not as a fluffy "dream it and it will come" tactic, but as a reprogramming tool to unhook people from the shackles of their past and rewrite the narrative of what's available to them.

A strong vision transcends mere goals or dreams. It's an articulate expression of what success genuinely signifies to you, in line with your core values, tapping into your strengths and resonating with your deepest desires. An authentic vision is aspirational and audacious, bypassing the question of *Is this really achievable?* It's the "more" minus the guilt or concern for capabilities and consequences.

If this is starting to sound unreasonable or overly idealistic, I get it. Trust me, don't ask my clients to come to my house and sit cross-legged in front of a posterboard and magazines so we can drink wine and create vision boards filled with expensive cars and clichéd affirmations like "You got this, king/queen!"

Jeremy was a high achiever with significant responsibilities. What I offered, like I do to so many of my clients, was a method to chart his path, to prevent unwittingly wasting time on distractions or detours. It was about aligning with his true self and desires, avoiding the emotional cost of resentment or limiting himself to modest visions defined by a risk-averse version of himself.

Jeremy looked directly at me. *"I want to speak. Like, travel the world and speak on stages. But I can't throw away everything I've worked so hard for in this job."*

I resisted the urge to ball my fist and punch the air in celebration. It was ambitious, but it was what we needed to launch Jeremy on the path to success. People often shy away from ambitious goals and desires.

And so do companies.

In my corporate role, we fell into this trap annually when setting objectives, avoiding ambitious targets due to concerns about year-end bonuses. More recently, corporations have recognized that tying employee compensation too closely to performance objectives discourages risk taking, creativity, and innovative failure.

I've applied this philosophy in my leadership roles, personal ambitions, and coaching, encouraging clients to pursue success beyond their initial beliefs of what's achievable.

So, let's begin with you. What do you truly desire if constraints were removed?

My goal with each client is to push them past their "I don't know," a knee-jerk response, a protective reflex that isn't true. It's easy to turn our backs on the often challenging journey to our dream life, claiming we're not sure of our desires. But each of us has a voice in the back of our heads shouting our wishes and protesting against choices that go against them, but we often muzzle it, shove it deep down, and hold ourselves back.

Think you're the exception? The one person who truly doesn't know what you want?

Imagine your best friend or a close family member asking about what you want: the big, expensive, lavish life; the job you believe you're unqualified for; or the hope to move overseas—whatever it may be. Do you get uncomfortable? Are you worried about being called selfish or delusional, thinking, *I don't want this person to judge me* or *What if I say it out loud and they hold me to it?*

So, instead, like Jeremy, do you allow "I don't know" to be the only thing to pass your lips?

This is a fear-based, protective narrative that dilutes your responses, masking your true desires with uncertainty. In my experience, people are very good at articulating their current reality and the truth of their situation. But this often includes emphasizing elements we don't want to exist. We can point out the negative aspects of our lives, the bad, the things that irk us, and what we suffer from every day; things like, *I don't like my job, I'm tired all the time,* and *I'm overworked.*

And these are all real and valid experiences.

But stepping out of our current reality and articulating our wants and desires for the future is another ball game that few have the innate ability to do. So, we call on the help of experts to coax it out of us. In coaching conversations, we try to bridge the gap between where someone is and where they want to be with what it will take to get there.

So, when the inevitable "What do you want to do next?" questions come in our coaching sessions, clients respond with the answer that is designed to end the conversation: "I don't know."

Moving Past "I Don't Know"

To move past "I don't know," we first need to realize that it isn't an acceptable answer. The words come easy and feel comfortable, but they're wrong. It took me a while to realize that for myself. But understanding this is the first step in the direction of your dream. Otherwise, you use it as a reason not to move forward. If you "don't know," then you come to a full stop because there's nothing further to do.

But even if you don't know the next step right now, you *will* figure it out.

Imagine you're in a supermarket looking for hot sauce. You can't find it, so you ask an employee where it is. They look you in the eye and say, *"I don't know,"* before walking away.

You're dumbfounded. An employee of the store doesn't know and just gives up? Their job is to figure it out. You wouldn't accept "I don't know" from a cashier when you ask where the hot sauce is. So why the hell are you accepting it from the *CEO of your life*?

So many of us give up when we don't immediately know something. We ask ourselves a question, and the first answer that bubbles up is "I don't know." Then we stop looking for our metaphorical hot sauce.

But you work and live here. You are the best shot at knowing the answer. And if you don't, you owe it to yourself to at least try to find out.

You need to use your resources to call someone, look it up, and use every tool at your disposal to discover what comes next. When we say, "I don't know," the immediate next step should be, *Well, fuck it. I can figure it out.*

Recognize that when you tell yourself, *I don't know,* it's a fear-based response. It's not true. This awareness will give you the willingness to dig beyond it.

So, when you say to yourself, *I don't know,* ask yourself, *What am I afraid of?*

Fuck it. I'll figure it out (or find someone to help).

I can't tell you how many times the following situation occurred when I was working my corporate job:

"Lauren, can you please step into my office?" my boss asked.

My heart rate picked up, and my mouth went dry. *"Sure."*

"We're giving you a new project; it's a SaaS project."

My first and immediate response was, *"Sounds great! Thanks for the opportunity."*

Then I would quietly retreat to my desk to quietly Google, *What is SaaS?*

It's because of countless experiences in my career and life where I've faced fear and uncertainty head-on that I'm a huge proponent of and can say, *"Fuck it. I'll figure it out."* As a project manager, I'm intimately acquainted with the feeling of "I don't know what I'm doing." But each and every time, I figured it out. And often, it was by leaning on others.

It's okay to tap into that curiosity and ask questions. If you don't have the answer, someone else does.

Curiosity should be the driver when you encounter the glaring red road sign with "I don't know" stamped across it. Curiosity overcomes fear. It's not a burden to ask questions; it's a necessity. So, fuck it. Ask, learn, figure it out. That's how we grow.

The Room

When we talk about moving toward your dreams and goals, we're not just talking about vision—we're talking about getting you into the *room*.

But what exactly is "the room"?

The right room doesn't just fit you—it expands you. It doesn't just recognize your strengths—it *dares* you to use them louder. It challenges you to bring your full self, not the edited version that's been trained to shrink.

And when you're in the wrong room? You feel it in your body before your brain catches up.

It's the Zoom meeting that leaves you deflated. The promotion that looks shiny but feels like a trap. The conversation where you smile and nod while your soul quietly exits the chat.

The right room feels different.

It's not perfect. It still has friction, challenge, stretch. But it also has *resonance*—that gut-deep sense of *this is where I'm meant to be*. It's the place where your values aren't just accepted—they're activated. Where your voice carries, your presence matters, and your weird, wild ideas don't need a disclaimer.

This room could be a boardroom, a classroom, a kitchen, a stage, a podcast, a studio. It could be in Paris or Pittsburgh, on Zoom or in a backyard.

What matters is how *you* feel in it: powerful, present, unapologetically yourself.

Because once you've experienced that kind of room, you stop settling for spaces that require your silence to make others comfortable.

And the truth is:

We outgrow rooms.

We build new ones.

We break the locks on doors we were never meant to stay behind.

So ask yourself:

Is the room you're in stretching you or shrinking you?

And if it's the wrong room, what are you still doing there?

The Power of Visualization

Our brains are always changing. With each new experience or situation, our brain figures out the best course of action and strengthens and weakens neural pathways accordingly. These experiences don't always have to be physical; they can be completely imaginary and still evoke a similar response in the brain.

Neuroscience studies have shown that simply imagining a threat results in almost the same response in the brain as experiencing it in real life.

Take that in for a moment.

Your brain reacts almost the same whether something is happening in real life or you're just conjuring it up.

Research suggests that one of the best ways to handle a threat is to imagine it, but without the negative consequences. It's a core idea in cognitive behavioral therapy (CBT), often used to help people overcome phobias. But here's the cool part: The same approach can be used to boost success. When you picture yourself succeeding or reaching a big goal, your brain reacts as if it's actually happening. This strengthens neural pathways linked to that success, a process called neuroplasticity. The result? Less stress, more confidence, and a serious motivation boost— making you way more likely to turn that vision into reality.

So, when you visualize, you're doing more than just dreaming—you're architecting your future, one vivid, imagined detail at a time. It's not just about "seeing is believing"; it's about believing so fiercely that you can't help but see it come to life.

More Benefits of Visualization

- **Boosts motivation:** When you take the time to really see your goals—like, picture them clearly in your mind—they stop feeling so abstract. They start to feel real, doable, even exciting. That clarity can light a fire under you, making it easier to stay motivated and actually follow through.

- **Programs the brain for success:** Here's the cool part—when you consistently visualize what you want, your brain starts tuning in to anything that might help you get there. It's a bit like when you decide you want a red car and suddenly see red cars everywhere. That's your brain filtering for what matters to you, and the same thing happens when you're locked in on a goal. You start noticing resources, people, and ideas that align with it. They were probably always there; you're just seeing them differently now.

- **Builds confidence:** When you imagine yourself succeeding over and over, something shifts. You start to believe it's possible. That belief builds confidence—and confidence makes it easier to take action, speak up, or go after what you want without second-guessing every step.

- **Improves focus and concentration:** Visualization helps you cut through the noise. Instead of getting pulled in a million directions, it brings your attention back to what really matters. You're less likely to get distracted and more likely to stay on course, especially when things get busy or overwhelming.

- **Get your head and heart on the same page:** When you visualize, you can actually feel success. You imagine what it would be like to cross the finish line, sign the deal, or reach that milestone. That emotional connection makes your goal more meaningful, and helps your mindset, energy, and actions all line up to support it.

Bringing visualization into your goal-setting process can be a game changer. It helps you stay motivated, mentally prep for challenges, and focus your energy where it really counts, making it that much more likely you'll actually reach the outcome you're aiming for.

Be in the Room: A Visualization Prompt

Having trouble visualizing exactly what you want? Grab a pen and paper. Let's walk through this together.

Close your eyes for a moment and imagine this: It's five years from today. You find yourself standing in front of a large, heavy door. This is no ordinary door—it's the entrance to the room, which represents your future, the space where your strengths, purpose, and values are fully alive.

Take a deep breath. You reach out, grasp the handle, and push the door open.

What do you see as you step inside?

Look around.

Thinking and speaking only in the present tense as if it's happening right now, what kind of room is it? Is it a boardroom, a studio, a community center, a stage? Is it filled with light, with energy, with possibility?

Who is in this room with you? What kinds of people have gathered here, drawn to your presence?

Now, look at yourself.

What do you look like? What posture do you hold? What energy do you bring?

Which of your strengths are being amplified in this space? How are they on full display?

What are you in this room to speak about? What is the message, idea, or vision that you are here to share?

As you speak, notice the faces of those around you. What do they see in you? What are they appreciating about who you are and what you bring? How can you tell? Is it in their eyes, their nods, the way they lean in to listen?

Finally, take a moment to reflect: What did it take for you to walk through that door? What did you have to believe about yourself to step fully into this room? What fears did you overcome? What permission did you grant yourself?

Open your eyes. Now, write it all down. Describe the room, the people, your role, your message. Get as detailed as you can. Not just what the room looks like, but how it feels to be in it and what challenges you overcame to get there.

These questions help trigger something called positive memory bias, which helps us feel more hopeful about the future by borrowing the examples of the past. When you narrate your future as if it's already happened, your brain can begin to wire those possibilities as real.

In essence, you're not just making up a story. You're creating a mental map that guides your identity into what's next.

And now that you've seen the room, you can't unsee it.

So, write it down like it's already yours. Because it is. (I'll give you space to do this in the next *Put It into Practice* section at the end of this chapter.)

Align Your Vision with Your Why

What is the key difference between an idea you see through versus an idea you can't seem to get off the ground fully?

The difference is your "why."

Being an entrepreneur is among the hardest paths I've ever walked. Daily, I grapple with the shadows of doubt: *Is my voice enough to be valued here? Can I trust my own instincts? What if my dedication goes unnoticed?*

We all have goals and aspirations, but do we really know why we're pursuing them? Without a strong sense of purpose, it's easy to lose motivation and give up when the going gets tough.

When I first started focusing on the growth of my business, I was heavily influenced by the work of Simon Sinek—a leadership expert and best-selling author best known for his concept of the "Golden Circle" and his TED Talk *Start With Why*, one of the most viewed of all time. His philosophy is simple but powerful: People don't buy what you do; they buy why you do it.

So, I turned that lens inward.

I didn't just ask, *What do I want to build?* I asked, *Why does this vision matter? What deeper truth, need, or desire is driving me? What's at stake if I don't do this work—and who am I becoming if I do?*

Those questions became my foundation.

Because the clearer I became on my "why," the more aligned, resilient, and magnetic my business, and my leadership, became.

I came to discover that my "why" is helping others become the change they want to see in the world. It came from a place where I wanted to look around and see more people who looked like me holding seats at the table. But now, more than that, I never want my son and daughter to look around and subconsciously feel limited by what they can achieve based on the color of their skin.

This is what keeps me pushing through setbacks, uncertainty, and rejection.

Discovering your "why" requires introspection and courage to confront challenging questions. Begin by exploring what truly motivates you at your core.

What are the principles and values that you hold dear? Consider the kind of impact you aspire to make in the world. It's vital to ensure that your vision transcends external achievements and taps into deeper internal satisfaction and congruence with your personal beliefs and values. By delving into these inquiries, you stimulate your brain's limbic system, which governs emotions, values, and motivations. This introspective process fosters a profound alignment between your daily actions and your core motivations, which is essential for achieving lasting success and genuine fulfillment.

Test Before You Invest

"I see the room, but I'm not sure I'm ready to go all in." Jeremy looked a little vulnerable as he ran a hand across the back of his neck. Now that he was being truthful and had voiced what he wanted, he was lost. He hadn't had to think this far ahead because he was convinced it would never happen.

I smiled encouragingly. Once a client overcomes their "I don't know" lie and identifies their first actionable next step (see the "Formula for Change" in Chapter Three), the notion of "test before you invest" is paramount.

It's time to do a test drive.

These test drives can take time.

Many people see the next step as an all-or-nothing leap, filled with fears of *What if I go all in and it's not right for me?*

I explained this to Jeremy. *"You need to date your idea before you lock yourself in a committed relationship with it. Like all relationships, your new adventure requires a series of small experiments to see if it's the right fit. You don't need to quit your job right away; first, sign up for a Toastmasters class. Get into the headspace of speaking and make sure you still love it."*

When I was first interested in coaching, the advice I received was to facilitate more within my company. I started facilitating director offsites and the annual strategy and planning sessions in addition to collaborating on projects with my sister. These "stretches" weren't my full-time job, but they allowed me to try something different and to realize that I truly wanted to integrate them with my life more.

If you're unhappy, find ways within your current role or situation to stretch and grow into the areas you wish to occupy. This allows you to test your interests while still enjoying the safety of a paycheck.

Curiosity can bridge the gap between where you are and what room you want to be in, making the pursuit of your goals feel safer. It removes the fear of *What if I make the leap and it doesn't work out?* and replaces it with confidence built through experience.

Putting It in Practice

Visualize your room

Close your eyes. Imagine stepping through the door into your room—the space where your strengths, purpose, and values are fully alive. Now describe it in detail below.

What kind of room is it?

Who is in this room with you? What do they admire about you?

What do you look like in this room? How do you feel?

What strengths are being amplified? How are they on full display?

What are you in this room to speak about or contribute?

How do you know others appreciate your presence and contribution?

Identify your "why"

Think about the vision you just described. What's your deeper reason for wanting to be in this room? Why does this matter to you?

What is your why?

Test before you invest

What's one small, low-risk way you can test your vision before going all in? When will you do it?

Receipts

You've done some powerful work in this chapter—and it deserves to be named clearly:

- You called out the "I don't know" lie—and got honest about what's *really* underneath your uncertainty.

- You learned how to move past fear-based responses and into action using curiosity and truth.

- You visualized your next room, not just where you want to be, but who you are when you're fully alive inside it.

- You started asking better questions of yourself, not "Is this realistic?" but "What if this is the map?"

- You confronted the voice that said, "It's not possible," and began replacing it with one that says, "Fuck it. I'll figure it out."

- You explored what it means to test before you leap— how small stretches can lead to massive clarity.

- You clarified your *why*—the purpose behind the vision, the fuel that will carry you through resistance and rejection.

You didn't just imagine a new reality. You gave yourself permission to build it. And you now have the tools to start— one decision, one test, one brave moment at a time.

Your Next Step

Ayyyy! Look at how far we've come.

You've stopped lying to yourself. You've named what you want. You've begun stepping out of fear-based stories and into intentional, identity-shaping decisions.

You've met your inner CEO, mapped your legacy, and envisioned the room that's calling you forward.

And maybe for the first time, you've said out loud what's actually true:

You know what you want. And you're ready to go get it.

That's no small thing. Because the real goal of this book isn't just clarity—it's claiming your power. And Part Three brought you right to the edge of that claim.

But now comes the next level of the work.

Because dreaming about the room and getting a foot in the door is one thing.

Staying in it, showing up fully, and thriving once you're there? That's where the real transformation happens.

That's the work of Part Four.

This next section is about what happens after the "aha" moment.

It's about navigating the realities of being visible, being first, being powerful, and staying rooted in yourself while doing it.

We'll talk about discomfort, resistance, backlash, burnout, and all the emotional tolls that come with occupying space you were never expected, or invited, to take up.

But you're not just here to enter the room. **You're here to own it.**

And I'm here to walk with you through every step of what that takes.

Let's go.

Part Four
You Said You Wanted the Room. Now Stay in It

FACING THE HARD OF CHANGE HEAD-ON

It's scary but
FUCK IT!

#BeInTheRoom

Chapter Eleven

When the Exit Isn't the End – Stepping Out of the Old Room

Blog Entry: What Have I Done?

08.21.2021 (two weeks after my family and I relocated from Toronto to California)

I'm not sleeping well. That seems like a logical starting point. To boot, I didn't come into this transition well rested. I worked right up until the very last working day before the move, and Chris hasn't taken a single vacation day either. The muscle aches from sleeping on an air mattress in our empty apartment merging with the stress-induced pain carried by my joints have taken a toll on my body. It's two a.m., and tears of agony are falling down my face.

I walked around the apartment in the dark, stifling my sobs so I wouldn't disturb anyone's sleep, before I landed on one of the four lawn chairs—the only furniture we currently have, which acts as my couch, my dinner table, and my office all in one. I picked up a pair of jeans to fold from the pile of clothes next to me on the floor, determined to find an ounce of progress and productivity when everything felt out of control. My fingers wrapped around the belt loops, I raised the crumpled jeans to my face and cried out the question I didn't want to ask: "What have I done?"

By making this move, I stripped away the things that granted me independence. No car. No bank account. No ability to earn money in this country, which means I rely on my husband for every dollar. I've lost all sense of routine and structure. My kids aren't in school or camp, so every moment I spend doing anything else is riddled with feelings of guilt because I've uprooted and then abandoned them. I've lost any ability to prioritize since everything feels so urgent right now. The kids, my new role, moving logistics, setting up a new life logistics, my coaching clients, and, oh yeah, there's me.

My dad referred to this yesterday as "buyer's remorse," and that pretty much sums it up. When you fantasize about something so much, you plan for it, and finally, you get it, only to wonder, Did I make a mistake?

I know that this feeling is rooted in fear. Fear that I won't live up to my sister's expectations when she asks me to join forces with her. Fear that I will not be able to provide my part of the income that gives my family the life I promised them on the West Coast. Fear that I am letting my husband down because he is having to shoulder so much of the relocation and household work. Fear that I am not being there for my children in the way they need me to be there for them. Fear that I'm not good enough to make it here.

Did I fail by coming here? If I stay, will I continue to keep failing?

———— • ————

Have you been here before? A time when you made a change in your life, whether it was a new job, a new city, starting a family, or launching a new business. You started off your journey with excitement for the possibilities, only to find yourself crying in the middle of the night, desperately searching for the eject button. Longing for the comfort of the life you left behind because even though it wasn't ideal, at least you knew it. You knew what to expect. You knew who you were.

At least in your old life, there was a pattern...a cycle.

But you need to find a way to maintain your resilience. Because the emotional turmoil you're experiencing is not only normal, but also almost universally predictable. Once we know what to expect, it gives us the permission and courage to embrace it with reassurance that what we are feeling now is temporary.

Understanding the Emotional Cycle of Change

Change, more than making decisions, is about navigating emotions, doubts, and triumphs along the way. Psychologists Don Kelley and Daryl Conner introduced a model called the "Emotional Cycle of Change," which breaks this journey into five distinct stages:

- Stage 1: Uninformed Optimism

- Stage 2: Informed Pessimism

- Stage 3: "The Valley of Despair"

- Stage 4: Informed Optimism

- Stage 5: Completion

We're going to walk through these stages together, and I'm going to show you how you can not only survive but thrive through each one.

Stage 1: Uninformed Optimism

This is going to be awesome. What could go wrong?

You're buzzing with enthusiasm for this new project or idea but may be blissfully unaware of the challenges ahead.

Action: Harness this energy, because it won't last long. Create a vision board or list the benefits you aim to realize. What's important here is that you clearly document what you are trying to accomplish, and you get very specific about why it's important, not only to you, but to those who will benefit from it.

Stage 2: Informed Pessimism - The Honeymoon's Over (and Now You're Crying into Your Google Docs)

What have I gotten myself into? This is way harder than I thought.

Sounding familiar? As you begin to take on the work and learn more about what entails in order to execute your idea, you become overwhelmed by the chasm of the knowledge and skills that you don't have. Maybe it's setting up a website, writing pitch decks, public speaking, or learning new software, tools, and processes. What the hell *is* all of this?

This stage is charged with negative emotions: frustration, anxiety, and even the desire to abandon ship. You're used to executing quickly, and now it seems everywhere you turn, there's a new learning curve to slow you down. This is where most people exit the journey. Self-doubt here is palpable.

Action: Revisit your goals, tweak them if needed, outsource your weaknesses where possible, and perhaps seek mentorship, coaching, or a supportive community. It's important here to build a support system so that you are not traveling this road alone. Because as hard as it is now, I regret to inform you that it's only going to get worse before it gets better.

Stage 3: The Valley of Despair—Yes, It's as Terrible as It Sounds

I can't go on like this. Maybe this was a terrible idea.

I'm going to spend a bit more time here, because the "Valley of Despair" is perhaps the most challenging stage of the Emotional Cycle of Change, marked by an all-time low in morale and energy. It's a point where it feels like you've hit a wall, and the light at the end of the tunnel seems faint or even nonexistent. All the good feelings you imagined feeling back in Stage 1 seem so far away, and you can barely recall what made you start this journey to begin with.

The feelings and respective inner dialogues during this stage can be immensely overwhelming.

- **Hopelessness:** "It feels like no matter what I do, nothing ever changes. Every effort seems pointless, like I'm just spinning my wheels and getting nowhere. It's as if the world is moving forward, and I'm stuck in the same spot, unable to make a difference."

- **Exhaustion:** "I'm so tired, not just physically, but in every way imaginable. My mind feels heavy, my thoughts are sluggish, and my spirit is drained. It's like carrying a weight that never lifts, a constant burden that saps all my energy, leaving me feeling empty and worn out."

- **Severe self-doubt:** "I can't help but question every decision I make. Am I doing the right thing? Am I good enough? It feels like no matter how hard I try, I'm just not up to the task. My confidence is shattered, and I'm haunted by a nagging voice that tells me I'll never be successful, that I'm just not capable."

- **Feeling of isolation:** "I feel so alone, like I'm in a bubble where no one can reach me. It's as if I'm surrounded by a sea of people, yet completely isolated. No one seems to understand what I'm going through, and I'm too afraid to reach out for fear of being a burden. This loneliness is overwhelming, like a silent echo in an empty room."

This is the stage where many give up or want to retreat. You might romanticize your previous situation and start to question whether it was really even that bad to begin with (kind of like an ex you keep going back to). Remember how excited you were at Stage 1 when you had a new idea? You're going to long for that feeling again and possibly convince yourself that you need to start fresh with something different, because *this* clearly isn't working.

Are you thinking about all those projects, businesses, or ideas you started and abandoned? I hope it's starting to make sense now as to why that might have happened.

If you recall my own journey, this was the moment where I felt utterly lost, grappling with a lack of financial independence and an overwhelming amount of responsibilities—moving logistics, setting up a new life, questioning my identity, my value, managing my coaching clients, and, most importantly, feeling like I was letting my family down.

Actions (there are a few):

- **Seek professional help:** This stage often takes a toll on your mental health. Don't shy away from seeking a coach who is trained to guide you through these dark times and help you see the next step forward. Aside from my husband, having a coach through my transition served as an invaluable guiding light that helped me tap into resilience and reminded me of who I was when it all felt lost.

- **Reconnect with your "why":** When you're in the depths of despair, you don't have to attach yourself to a brand-new idea in order to experience that optimism again. Revisiting your initial purpose can reignite your inner fire. Remember what you wrote down in the previous chapter? Remind yourself why you started this journey in the first place.

- **Set boundaries:** Emotional exhaustion often comes from taking on too much. Make it a point to set boundaries for yourself and communicate these to people around you. (More on boundaries in the upcoming chapters.)

- **Be kind to yourself:** Self-compassion is crucial. Acknowledge your feelings without judgment, and understand that you are not alone in this experience.

It's important to remember that the Valley of Despair is a phase, not a permanent state. If you're here—stuck in the dark, doubting the decision, and wondering if you're strong enough—I want you to know: this isn't proof that you're weak. It's proof that you're in it. And that matters.

You're already leading. You're just doing it scared. Keep going, because each small step forward will bring you to the next phase, and I promise, you'll like this one.

Stage 4: Informed Optimism—And You Were Worried. Pfffftt!

I see the light! I got this!

The tides are turning. Results of your hard work are beginning to trickle in and you're becoming increasingly confident and capable. You've been through the storm and survived, maybe even thrived.

Actions: Begin documenting your wins daily (no matter how small) in order to maintain your emotional high. Now might also be the time to pay it forward and mentor someone else going through their own storm.

Stage 5: Completion

I did it! It was tough, but I made it through.

Success isn't about the height of the mountain you climbed, but the internal and external barriers you overcame in order to find your way to the base of the next mountain. But don't be too quick to move on to the next challenge; take time to celebrate your achievements and express gratitude to those who've helped you along the way.

When we're initially inspired by a new idea, we may fantasize that there's a convenient shortcut—a bridge, if you will—that allows us to bypass the uncomfortable phases and land straight into the realm of success. While that might be true for more modest aspirations, if you're reading this book, chances are your goals aren't the low-hanging fruit. They're transformative, significant, and bold. For such monumental journeys, there are no easy routes, no shortcuts. Instead, you have at your disposal various tools and lifelines to aid you in your challenging ascent.

Expect Fear

There's no way to sugarcoat this: It's going to be *terrifying*. You will face fear and anxiety and question your sanity. And that's completely normal. You are not alone in feeling this way. Fear is a part of the deal.

If someone tells you it wasn't scary, they're lying to your face, or they are inhuman.

We're bombarded by people who seem to have mastered the game, saying, *"Just do it!"* or *"Be fearless!"* but that's not realistic. Fear is a signal. It tells you what you care about. Instead of trying to eliminate it, respect it. Understand that fear has a function. It can feel paralyzing at times, but once you start to see it as something you can tap into, it becomes a tool.

I don't strive to be fearless. I strive to develop tools to manage fear when it arises. Because fear is a companion that will always be there. And the difference between you and the people in the rooms you want to be in isn't that they've learned to eliminate fear or doubt. They feel it, too. They experience impostor syndrome; they worry about making wrong decisions, but they recognize it as a natural part of the process.

And I'll let you in on a little secret: the people you admire, the ones in the rooms you want to be in, have simply come to understand that fear is normal. There was a time when they were shaking in their boots, too. The difference is that they've developed tools, systems, and evidence from their experiences that they can draw on to reassure themselves that they can do the scary thing. They just do it scared.

When I was mapping out my transition from corporate to entrepreneurship, the to-do list felt like a monster. Every task, every milestone, seemed like it came with a side of *there's no world where this happens*. I was constantly teetering between excitement and straight-up panic.

But taped to my bathroom mirror, right above that overwhelming plan, was a single sticky note that became my mantra:

It's scary, but fuck it.

I saw it first thing in the morning and again before I went to bed. And every time, it reminded me that fear wasn't the enemy—staying stuck was.

There was power in naming the fear and choosing to move anyway. Not *because* I was fearless, but *because* I was committed. Courage, it turns out, doesn't show up when you're ready, it shows up when you say, *"Fuck it, we're doing this anyway."*

Anyone who's taken a chance on themselves has been in your shoes. They've faced similar situations, and they know how to navigate through them. They use that knowledge as leverage. Remember, it's about being equipped to handle the fear.

Building a Strong Community

There's no honor in being a one-woman show. At least, not when we're talking about building the life you want. We all need community, especially during times of transition. It's nearly impossible to navigate major changes alone, or at the very least, it's much harder. And why would you want to do it alone?

Whether you do it formally or informally, building a support network is key. Mentors, sponsors, friends, and family all play leading roles in helping you move through (and survive) transitions.

Mentors, in particular, are invaluable because they shorten your learning curve and help normalize your feelings. Often, when you're going through something challenging, you might think, *Is this normal?* And a mentor can reassure you that yes, it is. Their experience helps you realize you're not off course, and that reassurance strengthens your resilience. A good mentor reminds you to keep walking along the path. You're doing fine.

Coaches, on the other hand, have been a game changer for me. Whenever I felt lost or unsure of my next step, a coach helped me reconnect with who I am, what I'm capable of, and where my strengths lie. They helped me sift through the noise to find the next step that felt aligned with my voice, giving me clarity in the chaos.

It's also important to have friends in similar places. When I worked at my corporate job, I had peers who weren't exactly mentors, but they were my go-to people for venting and validating experiences. It was helpful to have someone to say, *"Am I crazy, or was that the dumbest thing you've ever heard?"* That kind of camaraderie, especially as an entrepreneur, is essential. Finding friends who understand the ups and downs and who are on a similar journey helps you stay grounded. It reminds you you're not crazy. You're not in this alone.

Surround yourself with people who are vibrating in the same direction as you. They don't have to be your mentors; they can be your equals, but it's vital that they're on a similar wavelength.

You weren't meant to build an empire alone. Find your people and let them remind you who the hell you are.

Putting It into Practice

Take a quiet moment. Write freely. Don't worry about form or structure. This is just for you. Close your eyes, take a deep breath, and ask yourself:

Which stage of the Emotional Cycle of Change am I in right now?

- ☐ Stage 1: Uninformed Optimism

- ☐ Stage 2: Informed Pessimism

- ☐ Stage 3: "The Valley of Despair"

- ☐ Stage 4: Informed Optimism

- ☐ Stage 5: Completion

What thoughts or feelings are most dominant for me at this stage?

What support or reassurance would help me most right now?

Imagine future-me on the other side of this. What's she telling me? What did she wish I'd known back when I wanted to quit?

What's one small act of kindness or encouragement I can offer myself this week?

Receipts

Let's be clear—you didn't just read this chapter. You walked yourself through the emotional trenches of change, called out your own fears, and likely saw yourself in one (or more) stages of the cycle. That's not light work. That's leadership.

Here's what you just did:

- **You normalized the hard part:** You stopped romanticizing success and started telling the truth about what change really feels like. No more pretending it's supposed to be smooth. Now, when the discomfort hits, you know it's not a sign to stop—it's a sign you're in the thick of something meaningful.

- **You located yourself in the Emotional Cycle of Change:** Remember "name it to tame it"? That awareness is power. You're no longer just reacting to your feelings—you're reading them like data. Whether you're riding the high of informed optimism or stuck in the Valley of Despair, you now have language to name it—and tools to move through it.

- **You faced the fear instead of bypassing it:** You didn't gaslight yourself into positivity. You looked fear in the face, gave it a name, and learned how to move with it instead of waiting for it to disappear. That's courage.

- **You challenged the fantasy of a shortcut:** You're no longer waiting for it to "get easier" before you commit. You now know that every stage has its purpose—and the only way out is through. The climb is where you build the muscle.

- **You gave yourself permission to need people:** You named your need for support—mentors, coaches, friends who get it—and dismantled the myth of the lone-wolf leader. Because we don't do this alone. We're not meant to.

- **You redefined what resilience looks like:** Resilience isn't white-knuckling your way through it. It's rest. It's clarity. It's community. It's sticky notes on your bathroom mirror that say, *It's scary, but fuck it.*

So don't underestimate what you just did here.

You didn't quit in the valley. You gathered tools. You told the truth. You kept going.

That's a receipt and a process worth saving. You might need to come back to it as you progress.

Your Next Step

You've stepped out of the old room, and while the ground feels shaky, you're not lost. You're in the messy middle, exactly where transformation begins. You now know that there are times when it feels like challenges are simply testing your strength or worthiness, and other times, it feels like the universe is literally screaming at you to get off the path and try something completely different. But how do you know which it is? Because being in the room isn't just about endurance. It's about knowing when to stay the course, and when to chart a new one.

I'm allowed to change my mind

#BeInTheRoom

Chapter Twelve

Winners ~~Never~~ Quit – Why Strategic Quitting is a Power Move

I hesitated to write this, let alone share it. This isn't a polished blog or a confident "lesson learned." It's more of a journal entry, a raw slice of my thoughts. When your livelihood is built on helping others navigate their path to success, admitting to stumbles feels risky. It's tough to say: *"Hey, I still struggle too. I still face failure in the very areas I'm supposed to master."*

But that's exactly why this chapter matters. The road to being in the room is ongoing, even for those seen as experts.

I'm no different. My brain is still wired to protect my ego, to dwell on the negatives, to scramble for safety, even when it costs me.

Facing the Moment: A Personal Journal Entry

11.15.2023

Fuck!! This isn't working!

I've spent two years trying to scale my business through an online course. Another ten thousand dollars gone. No return. Add that to the ten thousand for a marketing company's failed ads. Add fifteen thousand for consultants who "guaranteed" success. Add thousands more for copywriters and social media managers.

The hole keeps getting deeper.

I kept saying, Right strategy, wrong partners. But after the third failure, I couldn't point the finger anymore. Maybe it wasn't just the partners. Maybe it was the wrong strategy, or the wrong leader altogether.

As a coach, I know I'm supposed to embrace failure. But I don't get Fs; I get gold stars. That's who I am. Or who I thought I was.

If I'm falling this short, who even am I? And if my business isn't scaling, who am I to coach others?

Ego and Failure

Rereading these words, I'm struck by a thought: *How has anyone ever managed to share space with my towering ego?* It's a bit funny, really.

This reflection brings to mind a story from Ryan Holiday's *Ego Is the Enemy*—a cautionary tale about what happens when ego takes the wheel.

John DeLorean (founder of the DeLorean Motor Company) ran his car company into the ground through ambition, mismanagement, and arrogance. As failure mounted, do you think he accepted responsibility? Reflected on his mistakes? Course corrected?

No. He doubled down, orchestrating a sixty-million-dollar cocaine deal in a desperate bid to save it all. There's footage of him, baggie in hand, saying, *"This stuff is as good as gold."*

His company failed because of him. And his downfall deepened because he couldn't stop digging.

If only he'd paused and asked: *Is this who I want to be?*

While my misadventures haven't led me to a scandal of cinematic proportions, they do shed light on a common pitfall for high achievers: the existential threat failure poses to our ego. The notion of being intelligent, competent, and proficient is so woven into our identity that any hint of failure in these domains can unleash a torrent of anxiety, stress, and self-doubt.

So, you may ask, what was my next move? Well, for a while, there was no move. I felt gutted. I had been knocked down, and I stayed down.

When You Get Knocked Down, Stay Down

I once heard a quote that said, *"We don't learn from our mistakes. We learn from our reflections on our mistakes."*

Such a relieving perspective from the over-marketed path of overcoming failure and rejection. It's not a pep talk urging you to "just keep going." In truth, I find that advice misguided, despite its popularity on motivational posters.

Tim Grover, the renowned mindset coach behind basketball legends like Michael Jordan and Kobe Bryant, once said,

> *"When you've been knocked down, confidence gives you the patience to stay down for a minute, until you know how to get up better than you were before. Most people jump right back up because they don't want to look weak and damaged, and then immediately get knocked down again."*

This idea is about taking a moment to lie there, to really consider your next move, even if that means deciding to quit.

Reflection Point

Think of a time when you were "knocked down"—what would it have looked like to stay down, not in defeat, but in deliberate pause? Before rushing to your next move, what truths were waiting for you in the stillness? What might you have learned if, just for a moment, you stopped trying to prove you're okay, and instead focused on what you really needed next?

The Myth of Perseverance: Why Quitting Isn't Failure

In the pursuit of success, the concept of perseverance is often glorified as the ultimate virtue. We're told that if we just push harder, endure longer, and never give up, success is inevitable. But what if this relentless drive to persevere, to never quit, is actually leading us astray? What if, in certain situations, quitting isn't the antithesis of success, but a strategic pivot toward a more fulfilling path?

The narrative that quitting equals failure is deeply ingrained in our societal ethos. I say it to my kids all the time: *"You can't just quit every time something is hard!"* It suggests a lack of grit, a surrendering to obstacles, and a failure to withstand the test of resilience. Yet, this perspective fails to acknowledge the complex reality of our lives and careers.

Not all endeavors are worth the sacrifice required to see them through, and not all paths lead to a destination that aligns with our evolving values and goals.

Take this personal anecdote as an example. When I moved to Los Angeles, my sister invited me to join a local women's soccer league. Now, I've never played soccer beyond the occasional school scrimmage decades ago, but, wanting to spend more time with her, I said yes.

At first, I tried to embrace the discomfort. I was clumsy, out of place, and honestly pretty embarrassed. But I told myself, *This Is growth. This is courage.*

Weeks passed, and something shifted. Instead of feeling proud of trying something new, I found myself dreading Thursdays. I'd check my email, half hoping for a game cancellation. I'd mentally rehearse excuses. Don't get me wrong, it wasn't the hour on the field that gave me pause, but the hours of anxious anticipation draining my energy, creativity, and focus.

I had to face the truth: This wasn't just hard, it was misaligned. Improving at soccer wasn't connected to my goals, my purpose, or my values. My "why"—bonding with my sister—could be met in ways that didn't leave me depleted.

Quitting felt like failure at first. But when I let go, relief washed over me. I had reclaimed my energy for what mattered more. That's when I understood: Sometimes quitting isn't giving up. It's choosing what's right.

Blind perseverance can be a dangerous gamble. The "no matter what" determination to stick with a chosen path, regardless of the mounting evidence that it's leading nowhere or, worse, harming us, can drain our resources, diminish our well-being, and distract us from more viable opportunities. The cost of this kind of perseverance is measured in time and money, but more importantly by the toll it takes on our mental and emotional health.

Recognizing when to persevere and when to quit requires a nuanced understanding of our goals and the landscape we're navigating. It demands an honest assessment of the situation: Are we facing a temporary setback, or have we encountered a fundamental mismatch between our efforts and the outcomes we're striving for? Are we clinging to a specific path because we're deeply passionate about the destination or because we're afraid to admit that our circumstances, desires, or both have changed?

Quitting, in this context, isn't about giving up in the face of challenge; it's about making a calculated decision to change course. It's an acknowledgment that our time, energy, and resources are finite, and that they should be invested in pursuits that offer the greatest alignment with our current aspirations and values. This reframe from failure to strategic choice frees us from the sunk cost fallacy, the belief that we must continue on a path simply because we've already invested so much in it.

Sunk Cost Fallacy in Action

Looking back at my failed attempt to scale my business through an online course, I can clearly see how the sunk cost fallacy kept me tethered to a strategy that no longer served me. I had invested thousands on consultants, copywriters, ads, and marketing firms, each expense adding another layer of pressure to make it work. The more I poured in, the harder it became to step back and ask, *Is this really the right path for me?*

Instead of seeing each investment as a learning experience, I saw it as a debt I had to repay with success. And that belief clouded my judgment, making it harder to consider the most strategic move of all: letting go.

Reflection Point: The Sunk Cost Fallacy in Your Life

Where might sunk costs be keeping you stuck on a path that no longer fits? Consider these common anchors:

- **Time:** "I've been at this company for years. It would be a waste to leave now."

- **Money:** "I've spent so much on this degree, training, or business. I can't walk away without seeing it through."

- **Relationships:** "I've built so many connections here. Starting over would be too hard."

- **Reputation:** "I'm known for this work. What will people think if I pivot now?"

- **Effort:** "I've put too much energy into this to quit before it pays off."

- **Pause and ask yourself:** "Are these sunk costs pushing me forward, or holding me back from what I truly want?"

Unlocking the Freedom in Failure

Writing that journal entry was more than venting—it forced me to sit with the truth of my own missteps. And in that uncomfortable reflection, something surprising happened: I felt grateful. Not because failure felt good (it didn't), but because it made me see what I hadn't been willing to admit.

The strategies I'd been clinging to? The version of success I'd been chasing? They weren't for the person I'd become. They were for an old version of me I'd outgrown without even realizing it. That failure wasn't just about a course or a launch that flopped. It was a signal that it was time to let go of the identity I'd been holding on to and make space for something truer, something that actually fit who I was now.

And I won't lie, this kind of letting go is terrifying. It means stepping out of comfort. It means disappointing people (and maybe yourself). It means facing the unknown. But alongside the fear, there's also a strange sense of relief—a quiet freedom that comes from no longer trying to force what isn't working.

This wasn't my first encounter with this kind of reckoning. I felt it in my corporate life too—when I kept applying for roles that seemed like the logical next step, only to be met with rejection after rejection. At the time, those closed doors stung. But in hindsight, I can see they were pointing me somewhere else. Had those doors opened, I probably would have stayed in a life that wasn't truly mine.

That's the gift failure gives us, if we're willing to see it. It breaks down the walls we build around who we think we're supposed to be. It nudges us toward paths we were too scared to choose. It invites us to redefine success on our own terms.

Failure doesn't mean we're off track. Sometimes, it's the clearest sign that it's time to chart a new one.

Navigating the Crossroads: Do You Stay or Do You Go?

The decision to persevere or to quit is a crossroads we all face in our professional and personal lives. It's a moment that asks us to look inward, to assess our current trajectory against the backdrop of our deepest values and goals. But how do we make that call? How do we know when it's time to dig our heels in and push through, or to strategically bow out and redirect our energies?

Asking Yourself the Hard Questions

Here's your personal gut check. You don't need a coach for this, just your own honesty. Scan these statements and check off the ones that ring true for where you are right now.

- ☐ **This path aligns with my core values:** Reflect on whether the path you're on—or the goal you're pursuing—truly aligns with your core values. Are you chasing something because it's what you truly want, or because it's what you think you should want?

- ☐ **My sacrifices feel worth it to continue:** Consider the sacrifices you're making to persevere. What are you giving up in your personal life, health, or other areas that matter deeply to you?

- ☐ **My effort is leading to growth:** Assess whether your efforts are resulting in growth, both personally and professionally. Is there progress, or are you running into the same wall over and over again?

☐ **I am motivated by passion, not fear:** Examine the source of your motivation. Are you clinging to a path out of fear of failure, of judgment, or of uncertainty? Or are you driven by a genuine passion and belief in what you're doing?

☐ **I am being persistent, not stubborn:** There's a fine line between persistence and stubbornness. Are you continuing down this path because you're committed to seeing it through to a meaningful end, or are you merely reluctant to admit it's not working?

☐ **I've sought diverse perspectives:** Seek advice and perspectives from trusted mentors, friends, or coaches. Sometimes an outside view can offer clarity and help you see your situation in a new light.

Now take a look at the ones left unchecked. What might they be trying to tell you? Sometimes the boldest move is to pause, listen, and consider another way. The unchecked boxes aren't failures. They're signals. Indicators that something in your current path might be misaligned, outdated, or simply no longer serving who you're becoming.

And that's where strategic quitting comes in. Not as a last resort, but as a powerful, intentional choice. Let's talk about that.

The Power of Strategic Quitting

This is where the inner CEO you've been building gets tested. Not in the moments when everything's working, but when it's not. When you're staring at a failed launch or a half-baked plan and have to decide: Am I being strategic, or just scared?

Strategic quitting is not a sign of weakness; it's a sign of strength and self-awareness. It's about recognizing that our time, energy, and resources are limited, and you can choose to invest them in the areas of our lives that bring us closer to our true aspirations. By asking ourselves these tough questions, we can navigate the crossroads of perseverance and quitting with confidence and clarity.

Remember, every decision to change course is also a decision to open ourselves up to new beginnings. Each time we choose to let go of something that no longer serves us, we make room for something that will. This is the essence of strategic quitting: making tough choices that align with our deepest values and aspirations, leading us to a more authentic and fulfilling path.

Put It into Practice: Permission to Pause

Before you act—whether that be pivoting, persisting, or quitting—grant yourself something far more radical: grace.

This week, don't rush to fix or force clarity. Instead, carve out space for stillness. That might look like:

- A solo walk without a podcast or agenda.

- Writing a letter of forgiveness, to yourself, for the moments you held on too long or let go too soon.

- Naming one area where you can release the pressure to have it all figured out.

Your work right now isn't to make the perfect decision. It's to make peace with the mess of this moment, and trust that clarity follows compassion.

Receipts

Here's what you are taking away from this chapter:

- You gave yourself permission to stay down instead of rushing to bounce back: You examined the cultural pressure to "get back up" quickly and recognized that strength also lives in stillness, pause, and reflection.

- You reframed quitting from failure to strategy: You explored how letting go of misaligned goals or efforts isn't giving up—it's making room for what actually fits your values, energy, and season.

- You got honest about sunk costs and emotional anchors: Whether it's money, time, or reputation, you unpacked the weight of past investments and started separating what you've *already given* from what you *actually want* going forward.

- You sat in the discomfort of ego and failure, and didn't let it define you,

- You asked yourself the real questions—the ones only you can answer.

- You reflected on your own missteps not as evidence of inadequacy, but as signals pointing to growth, evolution, and next-level clarity.

- Through your personal gut check, you started to distinguish persistence from stubbornness, fear from alignment, and duty from desire.

- You began to see quitting not as a loss, but as a decision toward freedom.

- You started building the muscle to walk away, not with shame, but with wisdom. And in doing so, you stepped deeper into your power.

Your Next Step

If you're still here, it means you didn't throw the book across the room (I've done this plenty), which, frankly, is a win. You've done what most people avoid: slowed down long enough to ask the uncomfortable questions. You've looked your sunk costs in the eye, side-eyed your ego, and maybe even whispered, *"What* was *I thinking?"*

That's not weakness—that's wisdom.

Whether you decide to stay the course or peace out with two fingers up, just know: this journey isn't about proving how much you can endure. It's about aligning your energy, your time, and your *talent* with what actually matters to you now.

And your next bold act? Rest. Yes, I said it. Lie down. Put the cape in the laundry. Because burnout is where we are headed next, and as you know, burnout doesn't hand out medals, but it *will* hand you a nasty exit strategy if you don't take a beat first.

Being needed isn't the same as being valued

#BeInTheRoom

Chapter Thirteen

Did You Just Call me the B-Word? – Addressing Burnout and the Resentment that Lies Beneath

Before we go further, I want to acknowledge something important: this chapter is full. Full of stories, tools, and tough truths. That's because burnout is complex and deeply personal. I could write an entire book on just this topic (and maybe one day I will). But for now, think of this chapter as a map. You don't need to implement everything at once. Let the pieces that resonate sink in and revisit the rest when you're ready. This isn't about "fixing" your burnout overnight. It's about starting the journey back to yourself.

The Burnout Lie

When pursuing greatness, we all hit a wall at one point or another. Chasing success can feel less like climbing a mountain and more like running uphill on a treadmill that never slows down. No matter how hard we push, it never quite feels like enough. That little voice in the back of our minds keeps asking: *Am I doing enough?* And over time, that question gets louder, drowning us in guilt, self-doubt, and an ever-growing to-do list. We get stuck in this exhausting pursuit, convincing ourselves that constant grinding is just part of the deal, the price of admission for those who dare to want more.

And let's be honest: if you're reading this, you're probably someone who does dare. Someone who dreams big. Someone who has worked harder, reached higher, and carried more than most. Someone who has been told, directly or indirectly, that excellence is the only acceptable standard. That slowing down is selfish. That rest is weakness. That in rooms where you may be the only, the first, or one of few, you have to prove over and over that you belong.

This is why you are especially vulnerable to burnout. Because the bar isn't just high—it keeps moving. Because your ambition, your work ethic, and your desire to create impact have made you resilient, but they've also made you prone to ignoring your own limits. Because you've been conditioned to see your worth through what you produce, achieve, and sacrifice.

But deep down, we know this pace isn't sustainable. And yet, when it feels like we have to choose between financial stability and our well-being, it doesn't feel like much of a choice at all.

I know this struggle firsthand. I remember hitting that wall myself.

At one point, my career was taking off. I was a project executive, managing day and night shifts while juggling life as a mom with two little kids in daycare. My days were filled with three-hour commutes, late-night work logins, and back-to-back meetings. On paper, I was thriving—promotions, accolades, all the external markers of success. But behind the scenes? I was barely holding it together. I felt stretched thin at home, overwhelmed at work, and resentful of the imbalance in my marriage. No matter what I did, I felt like

I was failing someone: my job, my kids, my husband, or myself.

One evening, stuck in traffic, exhausted, and on the verge of breaking down, I caught myself thinking: *Maybe if I got into an accident* (nothing serious, just enough to force me to stop), *I'd finally get a break.* That thought was my wake-up call.

And then, right in the middle of all of this, I got promoted to director. It was a huge opportunity. I was one of the youngest people and one of the few people of color at that level in a massive company. But the truth was, I had nothing left to give. I took the job anyway, and the burnout only got worse. The constant praise I had received before? Gone. Instead, I was met with doubts about my age, my experience, my ability to handle the role. The pressure was relentless, and I was drowning in it.

Burnout doesn't usually crash into your life all at once. It creeps in quietly, building over time as you give more and more, only to feel like you're accomplishing less and less. And for people of color, there's an added weight: the unspoken (and often unrelenting) pressure to prove ourselves in rooms where our work is too often overlooked or undervalued.

There's a common myth that burnout is just a matter of doing too much—too many hours, too many meetings, too many responsibilities. But if that were true, vacations would cure us. Out-of-office replies would restore us. They don't.

Because **burnout isn't simply exhaustion. It's emotional depletion from chronically betraying yourself.**

Burnout comes from misalignment. From biting your tongue when you want to speak, carrying the emotional labor of being the "reliable one," the fixer, the one who just gets it done, and suppressing your truth just to keep the peace, hit the metric, or avoid disappointing anyone.

It's easy to point the finger outward. But more often than not, that resentment we feel toward others is really just misdirected resentment toward ourselves for the ways we've abandoned our own boundaries, silenced our own needs, or sacrificed our own joy in service of everyone else's comfort.

Let me show you what I mean:

- **"I resent my kids and husband for not helping me around the house when I already have so much on my plate."**

- *I resent myself for not asking for help. For deciding I had to hold it all alone.*

- **"I resent my boss for constantly piling on new tasks and ignoring how overwhelmed I am."**

- *I resent that I keep saying "yes" out of fear that "no" will make me look weak—or replaceable.*

- **"I resent my team for not stepping up the way I need them to."**

- *I resent that I haven't enforced accountability or made space for my own standards to matter.*

- **"I resent my clients for texting me late at night like I'm always on call."**

- *I resent that I trained them to expect that by never setting a boundary in the first place.*

- **"I resent the system for making it so hard to get ahead."**

- *I resent the ways I've contorted myself to fit into it, instead of building my own lane.*

Resentment is a signal, not just of being overworked, but of being out of integrity with yourself.

And here's the hard truth: **When you stay silent about what you need, you end up angry at people who didn't even know you needed anything at all.**

That's the burnout no vacation can fix. The kind that requires a radical act of self-loyalty.

It requires naming what you've been tolerating.

It requires grieving the roles you've overplayed.

And it requires choosing yourself, even when it makes others uncomfortable.

So what if we stopped seeing burnout as a sign of failure? What if, instead, we saw it for what it really is: a signal. A signal that you're dreaming big. That you care deeply. And that it's time to pause, reassess, and choose a better way forward. Because ambition and well-being were never meant to be at odds. They can, and must, move together.

Breaking the Cycle: Strategize and Empower

When I first started coaching, one issue kept coming up over and over: time management. My clients were convinced that if they could just master their schedules, they could avoid burnout, be more productive, and finally feel fulfilled.

So, if you skipped straight to this chapter hoping for a game-changing time-management hack, I have to be honest, you won't find a quick fix here. Because the real antidote to burnout goes way beyond calendars and productivity apps.

What I've come to realize is that better time management isn't about squeezing more into our day; it's about understanding the emotional forces driving our choices. The way we spend (or waste) time, the things we prioritize, and the tasks we procrastinate on all say something about what we believe about ourselves and our work.

This hit me hard during my coaching sessions with Stephanie, a high-achieving professional who, on the surface, had it all figured out. She was known for her dedication, high standards, and relentless drive. But beneath that success was someone teetering on the edge of burnout, convinced that her worth was tied to how much she produced and how perfectly she did it.

I still remember our first video call. Stephanie and her husband wanted to start a family, but she was overwhelmed. *"I'm already working sixteen-hour days,"* she told me. *"I just don't see how a baby fits into this. I think I just need more structure."*

Now, as a coach, I try to stay neutral, but even I had to smile at what I saw behind her: an entire wall in her home office turned into a giant whiteboard, neatly divided with blue masking tape into sections for priorities, deadlines, progress, and notes. This woman didn't need more structure—she had structure down to a science.

Instead, I gently told her, *"I don't think you need more structure. I think you need permission."*

And that became her real task: to figure out what permissions she needed to grant herself to make space for a family.

It sounds simple, but for Stephanie, it wasn't. She had to give herself permission to log off at four p.m., to be unreachable at times, to stop responding immediately to non-urgent emails, and—maybe the hardest one—to let go of perfection. These weren't just small adjustments; they were the foundation of how she defined her value. Her fear was real. If she let go, even just a little, would she still be seen as the high achiever she'd always been? Would she still be respected? Would she still be needed?

Her struggle is one so many of us can relate to. We chase better time management when what we really need is a shift in identity, especially as we grow in our careers and personal lives and start craving more. More balance, fulfillment, and joy.

For Stephanie, building the room she envisioned (a nursery, in her case) meant stepping away from the hands-on, task-driven role where she'd always proven her worth and stepping into a more strategic, empowering leadership style. It meant shifting from doing to guiding, from executing to delegating, from measuring success by output to measuring it by impact.

And that's the real challenge. You might think the hardest part is just changing how we work, but actually, it's redefining our value beyond the work itself.

This is where the *Cynefin* (pronounced kuh-Nev-in) framework becomes particularly relevant.

From Competence to Complexity: What Keeps High Achievers Stuck

Here's a hard truth for high achievers: Burnout doesn't always come from doing too much. It often comes from doing too much of what's familiar and measurable; work that makes you feel competent but keeps you stuck.

Cynefin gives us language for this. This Welsh word roughly translates to "habitat" or "place of belonging," and the framework, developed by knowledge management expert Dave Snowden, is a model for decision making that helps leaders and individuals understand the type of challenge they're facing, and how to respond.

But this framework isn't just for organizational strategy. It's deeply personal. It names why so many of us feel maxed out, yet stuck. It reveals why you might be constantly busy, but still not advancing.

Because truthfully, the work that once helped you succeed might now be the very thing holding you back.

Let's break down the domains, and what they sound like in real life:

Obvious (formerly Simple)

Clear problems with clear solutions. You know exactly what to do.

Examples:

- Responding to emails

- Cleaning the kitchen before guests arrive

- Reviewing someone else's work because "it's faster if I just do it"

- Folding laundry instead of finishing your business proposal

Why it's seductive: It's fast, predictable, and makes you feel productive. You get to check something off and feel the instant satisfaction of being "on top of things."

Why it's a trap: You stay busy but never make real progress. You fill your time with tasks that validate your worth without stretching your growth.

Complicated

Problems that require expertise or analysis. Not everyone can do them, but you can.

Examples:

- Fixing a process at work

- Running a launch or planning a detailed event

- Managing your household logistics like a project manager

- Juggling family finances, schedules, and obligations like a pro

Why it's seductive: This is where many high achievers thrive. You're respected here. You're the reliable one, the go-to. You know how to win.

Why it's a trap: These tasks give you recognition and control, but they also keep you buried in execution. You're always *doing*...but never stepping back to *design* the life or career you want. You become indispensable, but not truly empowered.

This was exactly where Stephanie lived when she came to coaching.

Her calendar was packed. Her work was flawless. Her systems? Bulletproof. And when life demanded more from her, like the desire to start a family, her instinct was to add more structure, more planning, more control.

But what she really needed wasn't a tighter grip. It was permission to lead differently, to rest, to expand into a new identity.

And that required a shift into the next zone:

Complex

No obvious answers. You figure things out as you go. Growth comes from experimentation and iteration.

Examples:

- Redefining your value as a leader who *guides* instead of *does*

- Delegating household tasks even if they're not done "your way"

- Saying no to something good to make space for something better

- Navigating a new season of parenthood or entrepreneurship without a clear rulebook

Why it's uncomfortable: You don't get instant validation here. The path is unclear, the return on investment (ROI) is delayed, and you might feel like you're not doing enough, or not doing it right.

Why it matters: This is where real leadership begins. This is where you build capacity, not just competence. It's also where you break the burnout cycle.

For Stephanie, this shift meant letting go of constant output and embracing influence instead. It meant trading in her "always-on" identity for one that allowed space, delegation, and yes—imperfection. That's when she finally had room for what she truly wanted: a family and a career she could sustain.

Chaotic

No patterns, no clarity, just crisis. Immediate action is needed to stabilize the situation.

Examples:

- A child gets sick and your whole week unravels

- A project explodes hours before a deadline

- You reach total emotional overload and break down in traffic

Why it's dangerous: You can't think strategically here. You react. You survive. This is where burnout peaks.

Why it matters: If you're always operating at this level, something's broken. You've ignored complexity for too long.

Disorder (the middle)

You don't know which domain you're in, so you default to what's most familiar.

Example:

- You feel overwhelmed, so you go back to over-functioning

- You're unsure about your direction, so you busy yourself with to-do lists

- You tell yourself, "If I can just get through this week..."

This is the burnout zone—where you're doing too much of what you know how to do, and not enough of what you actually *need* to do.

Here's the reframe:

You say you don't have time to think bigger, lead differently, or build what you really want. But the reason you don't have time is because you're buried in work that keeps you comfortable, but small.

The Obvious and Complicated zones reward your competence, but they don't require you to evolve. And for high performers, that's exactly why they're dangerous. You keep grinding, building resentment, wondering why the breakthrough still hasn't come.

Real change, real *leadership*, requires moving into the Complex. The territory where you don't have all the answers, but you're willing to grow anyway.

That's what Stephanie did. That's what I had to do when I left corporate.

And that's what you're being invited to do now.

Strategies to Navigate the Identity Shift

- **Reflect on your definition of success.** What used to feel like success, including checking off tasks and being the go-to problem solver, might not be the same anymore. Take some time to reflect: What does success look like in this new season? Often, it's about creating space for others to shine, making bigger-picture decisions.

- **Talk to people who've been there.** Talk to mentors, peers, or coaches who've gone through similar transitions. Their stories and insights can help normalize the ups and downs and give you perspective on what's ahead, and how to navigate it with intention.

- **Learn, learn, learn.** If you're stepping into a space where you don't have all the answers, that's okay. In fact, it's expected. Lean into the discomfort and approach it with curiosity. Growth doesn't come from already knowing; it comes from being open enough to figure things out.

- **Shift from doing to impacting.** Try zooming out. Instead of focusing on the volume of what you're doing, start asking: *What kind of ripple effect am I creating?* Think about how your leadership influences the team, the culture, and the bigger picture. That's where your real value lives now.

- **Be kind to yourself.** These kinds of shifts can stir up all sorts of feelings like uncertainty, doubt, even grief for the old version of you. Give yourself some grace. This is part of the process. You're evolving.

Because when you lean into an identity shift, you open the door to deeper fulfillment, more clarity, and a much greater impact on the people around you.

Work/Life Imbalance

Since I began coaching, I've spent a lot of time away from home—traveling across North America to facilitate leadership workshops with senior leaders and executives. And let me tell you, the mom guilt was real.

Even when I wasn't on a plane or in a hotel room, I was buried in my office—coaching clients, building the business, chasing impact. I was doing the work I loved, the work I felt called to do. But I couldn't shake the fear: *Am I becoming the career-obsessed mom I swore I'd never be? The Miranda from* The Devil Wears Prada? Was I lying to myself when I said I could have both a thriving business and a present, loving family?

Then came December 9th, 2022.

I had just returned from a week-long trip. The workshop had been a success, but I was exhausted. I dropped my bag in my office, trying to mentally prepare for the mountain of work still ahead. And that was when I saw them: a dozen pink sticky notes scattered across my desk, surrounding a handwritten letter from my eleven-year-old daughter.

The sticky notes read:

> *Do the best you can until you are the best.*

> *You are amazing and I bet you did something great today.*

> *Don't chase your dreams, RUN them down.*

> *And in the center was her note:*

Hey, Mom. If you're reading this, I'm sure you've found my sticky notes by now. On them, there's a little something to keep you going every day. Though I miss you, I'm so happy you got to experience what you did on both trips you took. You are and forever will be one of the largest parts of my life, no matter what happens. I'm so proud of everything you've accomplished these past couple years. You've come so far, and I think that you deserve happiness more than anyone.

Anyway, I just want you to know that you are loved and appreciated every day. Never lose courage because I know that you can do it.

– Love, Zara

I stood there, tears in my eyes and realized something important:

Balance isn't about being perfectly present in all areas of your life at all times.

It's not about giving 100% to work, family, self-care, community, and health *every* single day.

It's about seasons of intentional *im*balance.

There will be seasons where work takes the lead. When you're building, launching, pitching, delivering. And there will be seasons where rest takes priority; where family, healing, or personal growth becomes the center of gravity.

Trying to hold everything in equal measure every day is a recipe for guilt and burnout. But giving yourself permission to shift your energy with intention? That's sustainability. That's leadership. That's love.

That moment with the sticky notes was a turning point. Not just emotionally, but practically. It taught me that even when I'm not physically present in every moment, I can still be emotionally available and intentionally communicative. Embracing seasons has helped me maintain trust and connection with my family because they know what season we're in. I can say, *"This month, I'll be in a sprint, but next month, I'll be in rest."* It sets expectations. It builds boundaries grounded not in avoidance, but in love. And it reminds me that presence isn't measured by hours—it's measured by honesty, care, and alignment.

Back in my corporate days, I developed a quarterly rhythm that helped my team stay grounded and effective without burning out. It still guides how I work today:

- **Q1: The Surge** – We set bold goals and laid a strong foundation.

- **Q2: Streamline and Refine** – We assessed what worked, trimmed what didn't, and optimized our systems.

- **Q3: The Renewal Phase** – We made space for rest, travel, and reconnecting with family and friends.

- **Q4: Reflect and Envision** – We took stock of our wins and setbacks, and planned for what came next.

That rhythm gave us room to breathe *and* build. It helped us work smarter, grind less, and live more.

Because every "yes" you give is also a "no" to something else. And when you say yes to everything, what you're really doing is saying no to yourself.

That's why being deliberate about where your energy goes matters so much.

And that's the gift of honoring your seasons: it gives others a road map to love/support you better, and it gives *you* the freedom to lead without guilt.

Setting Boundaries for Your Time (and Why You Probably Won't)

I'll admit it: I hate how the word *boundaries* has become so overused in our culture today. It's been flattened into a buzzword, a catch-all, a slogan. And honestly? That makes the real work of setting boundaries feel harder, not easier.

When we hear *boundaries* now, it can feel entitled or privileged, like it's about drawing hard lines in the sand just because we can. We see a younger generation entering the workforce with BOUNDARIES practically tattooed on their foreheads, armed with long lists of things they won't do. And while I admire their confidence in protecting themselves, I also see how this can miss the point.

Because boundaries—*real* boundaries—aren't about saying no for the sake of it. They aren't about creating distance for distance's sake. They're about alignment. They're about creating the conditions that allow you to do your best, most meaningful work without burning out. Boundaries help you stay connected to what matters most, not become disconnected from challenge, responsibility, or growth.

And yet protecting our time can feel nearly impossible. Why?

Because setting true boundaries forces us to confront hard truths: That not everything we say yes to is actually worthy of our yes. Sometimes, we're complicit in our own exhaustion because it helps us avoid deeper, scarier work—like redefining our value beyond productivity. And mostly that boundaries don't just disappoint others; sometimes they disappoint the version of ourselves that believed we could do it all.

Boundaries are hard because they demand clarity, courage, and follow-through—not just the performance of self-care, but the practice of it.

Sure, we all agree with the "oxygen mask first" advice, but when push comes to shove, we're handing out our oxygen like it's going out of style. Is it because we're scared of looking selfish? Maybe. But honestly, that might be just the excuse we tell ourselves.

You've convinced yourself and others that putting everyone else's needs ahead of yours is selfless, but let's get real: constantly neglecting your own needs to meet others' demands is one of the most self-serving things we can unconsciously do—because it allows us to avoid deeper emotional work.

Remember the *Cynefin* framework we talked about earlier? Saying "yes" to everyone else's requests can be a perfect distraction, letting you tackle easier tasks that give you instant satisfaction. You get the pat on the back, the warm, fuzzy feeling of contributing, and it feels good. These tasks are in familiar, well-defined territories.

It also lets you hold on to the story that if you didn't have all these commitments, you could finally write that book, or your career would skyrocket. As long as you're overcommitted to others, you never have to step into your own full potential.

But here's where setting boundaries comes in, not as a cold, heartless move, but as a way to protect your time, energy, and, yes, your dignity. By now, you've hopefully worked on your vision and your "why," so it's time to have the courage to draw the line in the sand around what's yours. It's about valuing yourself by managing your time and not overcommitting. Protecting your time is about respecting yourself and your worth.

It doesn't have to be complicated or mean-spirited, either. When setting a boundary with someone, I use this formula: Affirm the relationship, declare your limit, and propose an alternative (when possible).

Got a friend or family member who's asking for your time? You might say, *"I always enjoy our time together and truly value our relationship. Right now, my schedule is packed, and I need to focus on my work and personal commitments. I won't be able to help you this time, but I can suggest someone else who might have the time to help, or we can plan something for later when I'm less swamped. Let's also catch up next week; I'd love to hear what's going on with you and share some updates of my own."* You get the idea.

In meetings all day? Try saying, *"I can dedicate thirty minutes this week for a focused discussion, but anything more will have to wait until next week."*

Project demands shifting? Assert, *"I'm committed to making this project successful, but the original deliverables were clear and agreed upon. If we need to add anything new, we'll need to adjust the timeline and budget."*

As you go after more in life and work, your role starts shifting toward empowering others rather than doing everything yourself. This is crucial for your growth and helps those around you step up.

It's normal to feel guilty or uncomfortable when setting boundaries. But think about it: You're not dismissing others; you're honoring your self-worth. So, would you rather deal with the short-term discomfort of setting a boundary or face the long-term consequences of not having any?

Ditch Your To-Do List: Prioritize Building the Room

Once you've set your boundaries, it's time to make the most of your "new" time and space to really move the needle on your goals and avoid burnout. And here's the thing—traditional to-do lists aren't going to do the trick.

To prevent burnout, the first step is to get clear on your priorities. Then throw out those to-do lists. They can actually be counterproductive, often leaving you feeling like you've accomplished less at the end of the day. Sure, ticking off "easy" tasks feels good at the moment, but those small wins often come at the expense of tackling the bigger, more important work that can really move the needle—the stuff you might be avoiding without realizing it.

Which brings us to a game-changing strategy: eat the frog. This one comes from Brian Tracy, a Canadian-American motivational speaker who said, *"If you eat a live frog first thing in the morning, nothing worse will happen to you the rest of the day."* In simple terms, it means you tackle your most daunting task first thing.

Spending ninety minutes to two hours each day on these "frogs" can change the game. This strategy helps you make real progress on your goals by addressing the stuff others might avoid or put off. It's about prioritizing what moves you forward toward the rooms you are building or want to be in, not just checking boxes.

My Exact Productivity Routine

Remember the Three-by-Three Challenge? I live that shit! At the end of each workday, I take a moment to align my tasks with my bigger goals for the month or season. I ask myself, *What are the two or three things I can get done tomorrow that will move me forward toward these goals?* This little habit helps me define what a successful day looks like, so I'm not left wondering if I've done "enough" for myself and my ambitions. It also helps me stay focused on the most important tasks, blocking out the distractions that aren't worth my energy.

By doing this in the evening, my brain starts processing these challenges subconsciously as I sleep. So, when I wake up the next day, the "frogs" I have to tackle don't feel as daunting. Sure, they're still gross, but they seem smaller and, believe it or not, there's even a bit of excitement to take them on and make progress.

This way of working ensures you're not just busy, but truly effective. It prioritizes tasks that move the needle rather than the ones that just make you feel like you're working. This is key in preventing burnout, because burnout doesn't usually come from being busy, but from feeling like your busyness isn't connected to something meaningful or bigger than just getting through the day.

When you set clear intentions each day, aligned with your long-term goals, you give yourself permission to focus when you need to and also to step back and recharge when the time comes. This cyclical approach reminds us that productivity isn't about constant hustle; it's about finding a rhythm that respects both the work and the rest we need.

In the end, achieving our goals is less about time management and more about managing our emotions, expectations, and the way we approach productivity. By setting boundaries, realigning our identity with what we're working toward, and being strategic about how we define success, we can pursue our dreams without carrying the weight of burnout.

When you reclaim your time, your energy, and your emotional clarity, you're building the room where your purpose can thrive.

Put It into Practice: Reclaiming Your Energy and Alignment

Burnout often signals misalignment, not failure. Use this worksheet to pause, reflect, and reconnect with what truly matters—with grace, not guilt. Write freely. Let honesty guide you, without self-criticism.

- ☐ Planting (visioning, beginning something new)

- ☐ Growing (focused effort, building momentum)

- ☐ Harvesting (celebrating progress, enjoying results)

- ☐ Resting (recovering, recharging)

Why do you feel this is your current season?

What needs your focus in this season?

What can wait?

Who might be impacted in this season you are in? What do you want to tell them/ask of them?

Receipts

This was a heavy one, but here's what you accomplished:

- You redefined burnout—not as a badge of honor or a failure of time management, but as a symptom of misalignment, emotional depletion, and self-betrayal. You learned that the cure isn't rest alone—it's radical self-loyalty.

- You confronted the difference between overwork and over functioning. You identified how familiar, competence-based work (Obvious and Complicated domains) can become a trap that blocks leadership growth and deepens resentment.

- You explored the **Cynefin framework** not just as a leadership model, but as a mirror. You discovered how staying in your comfort zone can become an obstacle to evolving into the kind of leader and human you're ready to be.

- You named where resentment has been showing up in your life and reframed it as a signal of where boundaries, truth, and healing are needed. You stopped pointing fingers outward and started reclaiming your power inward.

- You embraced the concept of **intentional imbalance**, recognizing that balance isn't a daily achievement— it's a seasonal rhythm. You gave yourself permission to thrive in one area while trusting that another can wait, guilt-free.

- You demystified boundaries—not as blunt instruments, but as expressions of clarity and care. You learned a simple, compassionate formula for protecting your time and energy without rupturing relationships.

- You shifted your mindset from productivity to impact. You stopped chasing busywork and started prioritizing the tasks that move your mission forward, even if they're uncomfortable (a.k.a. the "frogs").

- You walked away with a concrete, repeatable routine for staying focused: the **Three-by-Three Challenge**, permission-based reflections, and the courage to define success by progress, not exhaustion.

Your Next Step

You've named the signals of burnout. You've begun to see where overwork, misalignment, and avoidance have taken root in your life. You've faced the hard truth that constant grinding will not get you closer to the life or leadership you truly want.

Before you move forward, pause. Instead of adding another task to your list, give yourself space for reflection, grace, and forgiveness. Ask yourself:

Where am I pouring my energy in ways that drain me?

Where might I reclaim that energy for what truly matters in *this* season?

And as you move into the next chapter, remember this: Being in the room isn't just about having a seat; it's about creating a space where you can breathe, belong, and build without losing yourself.

But here's the catch that few people warn you about: As you claim that room, you may find yourself feeling more isolated than ever. The old rooms no longer fit, and the new ones? They can feel unfamiliar, even lonely.

How do you stay connected? How do you build relationships that support the leader you're becoming rather than the one you're leaving behind?

Stop shopping
for milk at the
hardware store

#BeInTheRoom

Chapter Fourteen

Who's in Your Group Chat (and Who Shouldn't Be)? – Navigating Relationships That Need to Shift—and Planting New Ones That Grow With You

Remember when Justin Bieber put out that song about having everything and yet still feeling lonely?

I know, I know. Quoting Bieber isn't exactly *Harvard Business Review*. But hear me out. The first time I heard "Lonely," my initial response was sarcastic: *Oh, poor Justin— life must be hard with all those Grammys.* But the second time I listened, I realized: I knew exactly what he meant.

Because really, success can be isolating. The higher you rise, the harder it becomes to find genuine connection. The people around you become less inclined to hear your struggles, let alone understand them. The very thing you've worked so hard for—be it respect, authority, or leadership— can also distance you from the people you care about or the people you *need* to know.

Success changes not just how you view the world, but also how the world views you. You're placed on a pedestal, often losing genuine connections in the process. Relationships may become transactional, driven by ulterior motives rather than genuine interest in your well-being.

That's what this chapter is about: not just auditing who you've outgrown, but learning how to build a support system for the next chapter of your life. It's about emotional honesty, practical boundaries, and opening doors to new rooms, without waiting for someone to hand you a key.

Don't Let Them See You Struggle

Feeling lonely is tough enough, but what makes it even harder is the fear of failing. Not so much because of personal disappointment, but because you don't want to let down the people who look up to you or depend on you. That pressure can make it tempting to keep your struggles to yourself, afraid that if others see you wavering, they might start to lose confidence in you.

This is something Barry Oshry, a systems psychologist and the mind behind the Power Lab, has explored in depth. His work, especially his theory on Tops, Middles, and Bottoms in organizations, offers a helpful way to understand how different roles come with their own emotional weight.

In Oshry's model, people in leadership roles (what he calls *Burdened Tops*) often carry the weight of their team's or organization's expectations. It's not just about making decisions and managing tasks; it's about being the steady, reliable presence others look to for direction and confidence. This can apply to leaders, entrepreneurs, parents...anyone in a position of authority. The pressure to perform, take care of others, and navigate challenges never really lets up.

And ironically, that weight can be isolating. Even when surrounded by colleagues, employees, or a strong network, leaders often feel like they have to keep their doubts and struggles to themselves. There's a real fear that if they show vulnerability, it might shake people's trust in them or impact team morale. It's a tricky balance to stay strong for others while still being human.

That's why understanding this dynamic matters, especially for those who find themselves in this role. Recognizing the emotional toll of being in the room can help create better support systems and personal strategies to make leadership more sustainable.

Are You "Trying to Buy Milk at the Hardware Store"?

Sometimes, we go looking for emotional nourishment from people who were never built to give it. That's what coach Marion Franklin calls "trying to buy milk at the hardware store."

This phrase captures the idea that looking for solutions in the wrong places is a waste. Sometimes we look for emotional support, validation, or understanding from people who aren't able to provide it, like asking for milk at a hardware store. Recognizing where and when to seek emotional sustenance is central in trying to navigate loneliness.

The antidote? Be intentional about maintaining and cultivating genuine relationships. Surround yourself with trustworthy people who can provide unbiased perspectives.

But the other element is embracing vulnerability. Opening up about your feelings isn't a sign of weakness; it's a sign of strength. When you're candid about the challenges you face, you create room for real connections that go beyond the superficial relationships that were likely created on the foundation of success.

Being in the room means you're not just changing what you do. You're changing who gets access to your energy.

Who Will You Leave Behind?

There's one particular fear that stands out for a lot of my clients: the fear of outgrowing the people they care about. The questions that come up in these moments are deeply personal: If I keep growing, whether in my career, mindset, or personal life, who might I leave behind? What if the people I love aren't evolving at the same pace? Will we still connect the way we used to? What if they don't understand or even judge me for changing?

This fear can be a huge roadblock. It's not necessarily about doubting your own abilities; it's about worrying what growth might cost you emotionally. The idea of outgrowing relationships or losing common ground with people you care about can make you hesitate, second-guess, or even hold yourself back.

I've had so many clients admit that they've slowed down their progress, or even turned down opportunities, just to avoid this kind of emotional friction. But the irony is, by doing that, they're also holding themselves back in ways that can feel just as painful. That what-if feeling, the lingering sense that they're not reaching their full potential, can create a different kind of disconnect with themselves.

So, how do we move forward? The first step is recognizing that this fear is real, but it doesn't have to dictate your choices. Growth is personal; it won't always happen at the same time as the people around you. And while it's natural to care about how your growth impacts your relationships, it shouldn't come at the expense of your own progress.

But the thing is, people don't just fall into "good for me" or "bad for me." Real relationships are more nuanced than that. And you need a framework that honors that complexity while helping you move forward with clarity.

Who Is in Your Arena?

When we go through big changes, whether in our personal lives or careers, it's easy to start sorting the people around us into two groups: supporters and non-supporters. Who's really in my corner, and who isn't? But that kind of black-and-white thinking can be a little too rigid. Instead, try thinking of your journey like a sports arena, where different people in your life play different roles.

First, there are the ones on the field with you. These are your mentors, coaches, best friends, family members, or even therapists. They're the ones helping you strategize, cheering you on, and picking you up when you stumble.

Then you've got the people in the stands. They might not be right there in the action, but they're watching from a distance, rooting for you as you go.

Next, there are those with tickets to the main event. They know what you're working toward, but they're more like occasional spectators. You don't necessarily turn to them for advice, but you still want to share your wins with them.

And finally, there are the people who simply aren't in the arena. Maybe they don't understand your path, don't support it, or even discourage you. And that's okay—not everyone is meant to be part of your journey.

Recognizing these different roles can help you manage relationships with more clarity and less frustration. Not everyone has to be in your inner circle, and not everyone's opinion needs to shape your path.

Who Goes Where in the Arena?

Figuring out who belongs where in your arena takes time, and a lot of small experiments. These aren't big, life-altering conversations, but little moments where you test the waters by sharing parts of your vision or struggles with different people. Their reactions will tell you a lot about where they fit in your support system not just based on how you think they'll respond, but on how they actually do.

How to Do It

Start small: Pick something meaningful to share. Something that matters but isn't so central to your dreams that a negative response would shake your confidence. You want it to be significant enough to get an honest reaction, but not so personal that it leaves you feeling too vulnerable.

Pay attention to reactions: Listen, but also watch. Do they seem engaged or dismissive? Encouraging or indifferent? Sometimes body language and tone say more than words. A half-hearted "That's cool" is different from an excited "Tell me more!"

Mix up your audience. Try this with different people, friends, family, colleagues, mentors, even casual acquaintances.

You'll get a more balanced perspective when you see how different circles react.

Over time, these small interactions will help you see who's truly in your corner, who's passively supportive, and who might not be the best fit for your inner circle. It's not just about who says they support you; it's about who shows it in ways that resonate with you.

Interpreting Responses

Enthusiastic Support (on the field with you): "Wow, that sounds incredible! How did you come up with this idea?"

These people respond with genuine interest, excitement, ask thoughtful questions or offer constructive feedback. Their tone is brimming with excitement, and they may even offer resources or connections to help you further.

Passive Encouragement (in the stands): "That's great! Good luck with that."

They offer general words of encouragement but don't care to go deeper into your plans. Their response is positive, but there's a lack of depth of engagement or genuine curiosity about the specifics of your vision.

Neutral or Noncommittal (ticket holders to your main event): "Oh, that's interesting."

These people might acknowledge what you've shared through a subtle smile and nod but quickly move on to another topic. They don't show excitement or negativity. Instead, they are polite and hold an air of distant interest.

Negative or Dismissive (do not allow entry): "Are you sure that's a good idea? It sounds unrealistic."

This kind of response often comes with skepticism, condescension, or a subtle (or not-so-subtle) focus on why your vision might fail. There's no constructive feedback offered, just doubt, fear, or dismissal. And it can feel like a punch in the gut, leaving you discouraged or second-guessing yourself.

But here's what's important to remember: These reactions often have far more to do with the giver than with you. Their response is usually a reflection of their own limitations, fears, or unwillingness to challenge the stories they've told themselves about what's possible. It may stem from their own experiences of risk, rejection, or failure, or from the ways they've learned to keep themselves "safe" within the boundaries of what feels familiar or acceptable.

For people of color, this dismissal can feel doubly heavy. We often navigate spaces where we've had to work twice as hard to prove ourselves, only to still have our aspirations questioned. The skepticism may not just be about your idea—it may be laced with unconscious (or conscious) bias about who you are and what rooms you're "allowed" to enter.

And let's not overlook the generational layer. For many in older generations—especially those who lived through instability, hardship, or systemic exclusion—dreams that stretch beyond what is "secure" or "practical" can feel threatening. Their instinct may be to protect you from disappointment, even if it means diminishing your vision. What sounds like doubt is often their attempt to spare you the pain they themselves once felt or feared.

So when you encounter this kind of response, pause before internalizing it. Ask yourself, *Is this truly about me and my vision, or is this about their fear, their experiences, their limits?*

Because the room you're building? It doesn't have to match their blueprint.

Don't Count Your Feelings Out

The way people react when you share your vision is important, but just as important is how you feel in response.

Pay attention to your gut reaction. Do you feel encouraged or shut down? Energized or drained? Did their response make you want to share more, or did it make you second-guess yourself? Your emotions are powerful clues about whether someone's presence in your life is fueling your growth or holding you back.

Also, notice how comfortable you felt. Did you have to downplay your excitement or tweak your goals to make them more palatable? Or were you able to speak freely, without worrying about judgment?

Tuning into these feelings helps you understand who truly supports you. If someone's energy and feedback lift you up, they're likely a good fit for your inner circle. But if you consistently feel exhausted or discouraged after interacting with them, they might not be the best influence on your journey. The people who leave you feeling motivated, understood, and excited are the ones who really have your back. At the same time, your reaction to someone's feedback might highlight a need for boundaries or deeper conversations.

These small experiments aren't just about figuring out who supports you—they also help you get more comfortable talking about your goals. You might even be surprised by who steps up to cheer you on. The goal isn't to seek approval from everyone, but to surround yourself with people who genuinely believe in you and your potential.

Setting Boundaries for Changing Relationships

Once you've taken stock of where people fit in your life, the next challenge is figuring out what to do with that knowledge. Sometimes, it means having an uncomfortable conversation: letting someone know that, for this season of your life, your relationship might need to shift. That doesn't always mean cutting people off, and it's definitely not about trying to change their behavior. It's simply about being honest about your needs and how your interactions might look different moving forward.

Boundary conversations are never easy. We often assume the other person will react negatively, so we avoid the talk altogether. Instead, we slowly adjust our behavior, hoping they'll just get the hint. Or worse, we don't adjust anything at all, which leaves us neglecting our own well-being.

I'd love to say I've mastered the art of being upfront with people when their role in my life has shifted, but the truth is, I'm still working on it. Sometimes it feels easier to avoid the conversation entirely. Rather than saying, *"I've outgrown the part of my life where your input is helpful,"* I tell myself the change is subtle enough that they won't notice, especially if we don't interact often. But when it's someone who was once a close confidant, the shift is usually obvious. And if it's not acknowledged, it can lead to resentment on their end, or mine.

In the last chapter, we spoke about the formula for setting professional boundaries in order to mitigate burnout. Let's expand on that formula in the context of personal relationships:

- **State the other person's value:** Begin by acknowledging the other person's value. It softens the message and reminds them that the relationship matters to you. Something like: "I really appreciate your perspective and the support you've given me in the past."

- **Be clear about your needs using "I" statements:** Then, gently but firmly, state your boundary. Framing it from your own experience makes it feel less like a rejection and more like a reflection of where you are: "...but I've realized I need to focus on my new business venture, which is taking a lot of my time and energy right now."

- **Offer an alternative (if possible):** If it makes sense, propose another way to stay connected. That way, you're not closing a door. Instead, you're finding a new one that works better for you: "I won't be able to make our regular social gatherings for a while, but I'd love to catch up over a quick coffee every now and then."

Putting it all together, it might sound like this: *"I really appreciate your perspective and the support you've given me in the past. But I've realized I need to focus on my new business venture, which is taking a lot of my time and energy. I won't be able to make our regular hangouts for a bit, but I'd love to grab a coffee when we can."*

This way, you're being honest and respectful. You're protecting your energy and keeping the relationship intact. It's not always easy, but it gets easier with practice.

Besides, you're going to need some of that energy for what's coming next.

You didn't think I'd have a whole chapter on relationships and not talk about networking, did you?

And before you decide to skip this next part because you *hate* networking (I mean, who doesn't?), I'm going to remind you that you picked up this book because you wanted to stretch yourself outside of your comfort zone in order to change your reality. Soooooo...limber up, because we are stretching.

Getting into New Rooms: Stop Waiting to Be Invited

I know why networking gets a bad reputation.

The thought of walking into a room full of strangers, balancing a lukewarm glass of white wine in one hand and your carefully rehearsed elevator pitch in the other, is exhausting. It can feel transactional, inauthentic, and, let's be honest, a little desperate.

That's because most traditional networking advice is based on outdated rules telling us to treat relationships like a numbers game: collect as many business cards as you can, follow up fast, and hope one of them pays off. It's speed dating in a blazer.

But *real* networking—the kind that opens doors to new rooms—isn't about how many people you know. It's about how deeply and intentionally you're connected to the right people.

And more importantly, it's about how you show up in those relationships—with clarity, purpose, and generosity.

Most people hate networking because they've been taught to perform instead of connect. They're taught to seek visibility instead of alignment. They're taught to impress instead of offer value. And that's where this chapter takes a different turn.

I'm not talking about networking. I'm talking about *connecting*.

Most people overcomplicate networking. They think it's reserved for the extroverted, the ultra-polished, the people with perfect LinkedIn profiles and a Rolodex of impressive contacts. They believe getting into new rooms, including new industries and opportunities, is about proving your worth from a distance and hoping someone notices.

That doesn't work. New rooms open because someone remembers your name when the door is unlocked. And for that to happen, you need to be on their mental Rolodex.

The Coffee Chat That Changed a Career

When I was a director, I led teams across multiple provinces. Part of my effort to build relationships was visiting local offices, not just to lead, but to listen.

On one of these visits to Ottawa, I received an email from a frontline team member—not even my direct report, but one layer below:

I know you're going to be very busy, but I was hoping we could grab a coffee while you're here. Totally okay if it's not possible this time.

It hit me like a punch to the gut. Not because of the ask, but because I recognized the *story* underneath it.

She assumed I was too busy, senior, to make time for someone in her role. And I knew that story intimately, because I'd told it to myself a hundred times when I was earlier in my career. I just couldn't believe that I had reached a point in my career where someone thought it of *me*.

We met for coffee.

She shared her current role, and then opened up about the skills she wanted to grow and the areas of the business she was curious about. I listened, nodded, appreciated her clarity, but I didn't know what to do with that information at the time.

Fast-forward two months: a former team member of mine was building a new department and looking for a specific skillset. As he described what he needed, the connection clicked immediately.

"I know someone you should talk to."

That five-minute email and thirty-minute coffee led to a promotion, a new opportunity, and the exact kind of role she had described to me. One she may never have heard about otherwise.

Here's the point:

She wasn't in the room where her name came up, but her courage got her in.

I took that lesson and applied it to myself when I was exploring a transition within my company. I reached out to people both in my network, and people who weren't in my network but were leading teams I was curious about.

The purpose: I needed to get on as many mental Rolodexes as possible. I knew that I couldn't advocate for myself in all the rooms, but I could find ways to be brought into rooms that I couldn't yet access through others.

The same applied when I was beginning to build my coaching business.

I booked time with every coach I could get access to. I asked how they started, what mistakes they made, what they'd do differently. I didn't have a pitch, but I did I have questions.

And guess what? Every single conversation built clarity, confidence, and, yes, connections. Because I wasn't waiting to be invited—I was building the room myself.

Why This Matters: Dunbar's Number

According to anthropologist Robin Dunbar, humans can only maintain around 150 stable relationships at a time. That includes people you know personally, trust, and stay in touch with.[5]

When someone is thinking about whom to promote, whom to partner with, whom to recommend, or whom to refer, they're scanning their 150.

Do you see now why people are spending hours upon hours on golf courses? It's not leisure, like you might assume— it's strategy. That's where mental Rolodexes are curated. Proximity builds familiarity, and familiarity builds access.

For years, golf has operated as a kind of unofficial boardroom, especially for those who've historically held

5   Dunbar, R. I. M. (2021, May 13). *Robin Dunbar explains why his "number" still counts.* Social Science Space. https://www.mckinsey.com/women-in-the-workplace-2024

power. But that doesn't mean you need to pick up a nine iron. It just means you need to be intentional about where, and with whom, you're showing up.

Sure, it wasn't on a fairway, but without that coffee chat, I can honestly say that employee of mine would not have been on my 150 radar.

So the question becomes: Are you on the right people's radar? Are you in the room, even when you're not in the room?

Let's break the myth that you'll be invited into new rooms once you're "ready" or "worthy."

More often, you get in because:

- You asked thoughtful questions.

- You expressed genuine curiosity.

- You made your value visible. Maybe not perfectly, but consistently.

- You asked for the coffee.

Visibility is not vanity. It's strategy. And relationship building isn't about collecting people—it's about connecting purposefully.

What It Takes to Get in the Room

Here's what I've learned after decades in corporate and entrepreneurship: Getting into new rooms doesn't require a title or a referral. It requires action. Here's how:

- **Be strategic with your energy**: Apply Dunbar's insight: your brain can't manage more than ~150 people. So ask: *Who is taking up space in my circle that doesn't belong in my next chapter?*

- **Make space for new, strategic relationships that stretch you forward:** Make the Ask. Stop assuming you're bothering people. Most people are happy to talk about themselves. One coffee chat can change your trajectory. If someone had a role in shaping the room you want to enter, reach out.

- **Get on their mental Rolodex:** Be memorable, not flashy. Share your goals. Ask about theirs. Offer value—today or someday. Forget about a pitch; you just need alignment.

- **Speak your goals out loud:** That team member got promoted not just because she was smart, but because she told someone what she wanted. The world can't help you if you never say what you're aiming for.

Put It into Practice: Relationship Mapping

We often think of our networks as static, consisting of people we've worked with, grown up with, or know socially. But if you're building a new room, your relationships need to evolve alongside your goals. This exercise will help you assess where your relationship energy is going and where it needs to go next.

Remember: This is not about cutting people off—it's about **intention**. You only get around 150 meaningful connection slots (thanks, Dunbar), so spend them wisely.

Step 1: Clarify your new room

Before mapping relationships, **name the room** you're stepping into. Is it a new industry? A leadership role? Entrepreneurship? A new version of yourself?

(Example: I want to transition into consulting and get on panels about inclusive leadership.) My goal/new room:

Tip: Refer to the visualization prompt you did in Chapter Nine.

Step 2: Audit your energy

Who are three people you're spending energy on who aren't aligned with your next chapter?

1.

2.

3.

What boundaries need to shift?

Step 3: Identify opportunity connectors

Who are three people already in rooms you want to be in?

1.

2.

3.

How might you reconnect and/or offer value?

Step 4: Plant new seeds

Who are three people you don't know yet but would love to learn from, collaborate with, or be referred by?

1.

2.

3.

Step 5: Take one bold action

Pick one name from your map and take one of these simple steps:

- Send a message asking for a twenty-minute coffee chat

- Share something valuable with them (an article, opportunity, insight)

- Offer support on a project they care about

- Post publicly about the room you're building and tag them in a comment or DM

The goal isn't to "network." The goal is to connect with purpose.

Receipts

You did deep, honest work in this chapter, and you probably felt it. Let's recap what you just navigated:

- You faced the emotional weight of leadership: You named how success, authority, and ambition can bring loneliness, and recognized that being at the top doesn't mean you have to carry it all alone.

- You stopped looking for milk at the hardware store: You started auditing where you're going for validation, support, or encouragement—and whether those sources are even capable of giving you what you nee

- You redefined loyalty and outgrowing people: Instead of guilt-tripping yourself about leaving people behind, you started to honor the truth that not everyone can come with you, and that doesn't make you a villain.

- You mapped out your support system: You got clear about who's in your arena: who's on the field with you, who's in the stands, and who might need to move outside the arena for your own peace.

- You practiced how to communicate boundaries with care: You learned a script and structure for having difficult, respectful conversations when your needs in a relationship change.

- You reframed the "ick" out of networking: You stopped seeing it as a dirty word and started treating it like what it really is: connection, alignment, and courage to put yourself on someone's radar—with purpose.

- You realized it's not about proving your worth: It's about planting seeds, offering value, and being visible in rooms that match the next version of who you're becoming.

Your Next Step

Before we move forward, take a moment to acknowledge what you've done.

Seriously, take a moment.

If you've made it this far, you've done the work that most people avoid. You've faced the difficult narratives this book has challenged you to confront: through Part One (where you began to question the rooms you've occupied), Part Two (where you examined how you've been shaped by those rooms), Part Three (where you dared to envision what more could look like), and especially Part Four, where you've stared down the isolation, the fear of outgrowing others, and the complicated emotions that come with stepping into your own power.

This is the hard work. The work that few choose to do.

Because honestly? Most people live by a story that says, *You're here to do what you* have *to do. Doing what you* want *to do, and living and leading authentically, doesn't pay the bills.* That story keeps them stuck in rooms that no longer fit. They end up chasing validation or security, even when it costs them their joy, their energy, their very sense of self.

You're doing the work that saves you from that cost.

Because the cost of not doing this work is steep:

- A life where you achieve all the external markers of success, but feel empty inside.

- A life where you're surrounded by people, but feel unseen.

- A life where you're busy but not fulfilled.

And here's the final, important truth as you stand at this threshold: Clarity means nothing without action.

You've uncovered what matters. You've started to see what's possible. But seeing is not the same as stepping in. And that's where we go next.

This next chapter isn't about *who* will let you in—it's about how you'll show up once you're there.

Part Five
Be In The Room

TAKING UP SPACE AND
HOW YOU LET YOURSELF BE SEEN

I give myself
permission to
be messy

#BeInTheRoom

Chapter Fifteen
It's On You Now – Overcoming Self-Sabotaging Behaviors

The Self-Sabotage Spiral

Picture this: It's year two of running my coaching business, and I'm full-on spiraling at the kitchen table. Like, meltdown-mode spiraling. My voice is shaky and I'm drowning in comparison and caffeine.

"I should be further by now," I barked at my husband, pacing like a feral raccoon. *"I should've grown faster. I don't even know what the hell I'm supposed to do next because everything I've already tried isn't working!"*

I said it like I was expecting him to pull a miracle out of the cutlery drawer.

He looked at me—calm, sweet, maddeningly supportive—and gently laid one hand on my knee. He met my eyes and said, with deep sincerity:

"Whatever you need to do, Lauren. I support you."

I'm sure he was expecting a Hallmark movie moment where I would stare back into his eyes with gratitude. Tears of despair converted into tears of love. Overwhelmed with all the emotions that come with remembering why I decided to marry this perfect human sitting before me.

But is that what happened? Nope!

My eyes centered on him with absolute rage right before I *lost* it.

"How dare you?!" I snapped. *"How dare you give me full support and permission?! Now I can't even blame you if this shit doesn't work out. It's all on me, asshole!"*

We stared at each other, me fuming, him blinking slowly like I'd just kicked a puppy.

And that was when it hit me. This wasn't about business strategy. It was about self-permission.

I wanted to blame someone. I wanted to point the finger when things got hard. I wanted a clean, easy out.

I mean, would it have been so hard to say, "You know what, Lauren, I think this little experiment is over. Let's dust off that IT resume"?

But he had the audacity to hand me *full* autonomy.

And I wasn't ready for it.

We waste an *absurd* amount of time waiting for external permission. Permission from our boss, our parents, our mentors, our partner, the mysterious council of "people who know better." We wait for a nod, a green light, a sign from the universe, an Instagram post that aligns perfectly with our self-doubt.

But at some point, you realize that **external permission doesn't do anything without self-permission.** Even when others believe in us, advocate for us, or open doors on our behalf, if we haven't claimed it for ourselves, we'll find a way to stall. We'll sabotage, overthink, shrink, deflect, or wait for a "better time."

Why? Because self-permission means **it's on you now.** No more hiding behind "they didn't give me a chance." No more waiting for someone else to initiate the risk.

Everyone wants to feel that someone is holding the door open for them, but simply knowing the door is open isn't enough to propel us into the room we're meant to be in.

You are the initiator now. And that's terrifying. But it's also liberating as hell.

Being in the room doesn't just mean physically showing up; it means being willing to take up space, mess and all. This chapter is your permission slip to do exactly that.

How to Give Yourself Permission

Self-permission goes beyond overcoming limiting beliefs; it's a powerful tool in that process. My first real encounter with self-permission happened during my coaching school days. Practice groups often triggered my fears and limiting beliefs—the fear of making mistakes or failing.

Then one of my teachers shared a game-changing piece of advice: *"Give yourself permission to be messy."*

As a high achiever with a type-A personality, this idea was revolutionary. I had always strived for perfection, especially in front of others. Allowing myself to be imperfect and vulnerable had never crossed my mind.

Those words triggered a shift within me. By giving myself permission to be messy, I realized my limiting beliefs held less power over me. I accepted that it was okay not to have everything figured out perfectly. I could show up authentically without the constant pressure to perform flawlessly.

That moment marked my introduction to the transformative power of self-permission.

I began applying this principle whenever fear or doubt surfaced. It became a method of confronting my fears head-on: *What am I most afraid of? Can I give myself permission to embody that fear, to embrace the messiest and most uncertain version of myself?*

Because once you grant yourself permission to be that which you fear most, what's left to hold you back?

One effective strategy is to seek out examples of people who are already doing what you aspire to do. When I was starting out, seeing people who looked like me succeeding was pivotal. It shattered the limiting belief that success was reserved for a certain profile. It's hard to have the limiting belief of "people who don't look like me don't find success or aren't able to break through" when you step into rooms where there are fifty-two examples proving you wrong. Then you realize you can't believe it anymore, and so ultimately, what more can you do but grant yourself permission to try?

Three Ways You Might Be Self-Sabotaging

All this being said, sometimes we get in the way of our own self-permission. We sabotage. And it's frustrating because we know we're doing it, but can't seem to stop ourselves.

There's science that distinguishes a few types of saboteurs. However, in my experience as a coach, I've seen the range and can sum them up into the three most common ones among high achievers: the Perfectionist, the Hypervigilant, and the Scorekeeper (a.k.a. the Hyper-Achiever). But what do these really mean?

The Perfectionist: Too often, I hear people say "I'm a perfectionist" and wear it as a sort of badge. Let's get something straight: Perfectionism isn't a flex. It's not a personality quirk, a leadership strength, or some gold-plated proof that you just "care more than others." It's fear in a really convincing outfit.

I know, I know—that stings. But I'm saying it because I've been there. And I've coached enough high achievers to know **the difference between excellence and perfectionism.**

Perfectionism is a form of emotional procrastination. The idea that *if I can just get it right, I won't feel rejection shame or discomfort.* It sounds like:

- "It's not ready yet."

- "I just need to tweak one more thing."

- "I'll start once I've done more research."

- "I don't want to look unprofessional."

273

- "This needs to be absolutely right before I put it out."

As you can see, perfectionism masquerades as high standards, but let's call it what it is: Control. Delusion. Delay. The lie that you need to be flawless to be worthy.

Meanwhile, excellence is about taking responsibility for the outcome, not the illusion of control. It means releasing work that's complete, even if it's not perfect because you know that *real* growth lives in iteration, feedback, and action. It sounds like:

Excellence is:

- Execution over excuses.

- Releasing work that's complete, even if it's not perfect.

- Taking responsibility for the outcome, not the illusion of control.

- Knowing that real growth lives in iteration, feedback, and action.

Excellence doesn't fear failure—it requires **it**

- "It's good enough to test/start."

- "I'll improve it after I get real-world feedback."

- "Done is better than perfect—because perfect never arrives."

Excellence moves. It builds. It adapts. All the while, perfectionism is editing the same sentence forty-seven times and still never hits publish.

Even in my own business, there are endless opportunities for me to show up "perfectly": the Instagram content, the course modules, this book you're reading—they all could be "better," right? That's where the trap is.

While we work toward perfection, we build our own impossible standards. When we don't put work out there, guess what? We miss the vital feedback from the people that actually matter: my audience, my clients, my customers. You.

Self-Permission: "I give myself permission to ship, to learn out loud, and to improve through action. I don't need to be perfect to be valuable."

This is why early on in my entrepreneurial journey, I wrote some of the best advice I'd heard on every one of my notebooks and stuck it on a sticky note on each of my mirrors. Guy Kawasaki, who was a marketing specialist and one of the Apple employees responsible for marketing their Macintosh computer line in 1984, said: *"Lots of things made the first Mac in 1984 a piece of crap, but it was a revolutionary piece of crap. Revolutionary means you ship and then test..."*

That's why I keep sticky notes on my mirrors, not because I'm into self-help clichés, but because sometimes your reflection needs a reminder that *done* is better than *perfect*.

When I work with my clients, I push them to move up their internal deadlines because most times, those deadlines let perfection take priority. Does this mean I push my clients to be sloppy? No. They couldn't be sloppy even if they tried. It's not in their DNA. I push them to lower the voice of their internal critic, to make room for the feedback coming from external sources.

What we're looking for is momentum, growth. We're looking to get out there and actually do something. You put in the work, you ship it, and then you listen. You take the feedback, you adjust, you adapt.

That's how you refine, grow, and how you create excellence.

The Hypervigilant: When you're stuck in this saboteur mindset, your brain is basically on high alert, constantly scanning for potential threats. It's like your fight-or-flight response is stuck in overdrive. At one point, it was a survival instinct that made sense when we were dodging predators, but not so much in today's world. The problem is, when this hypervigilance is always switched on, it can spiral into stress and anxiety.

For women of color, this can be even more intense because of societal pressures and prejudices. I've seen it in my clients—walking into a room and immediately assessing safety, like finding familiar faces or a welcoming vibe. If they don't, it feels like they're wearing a target, thanks to the systemic expectation to be twice as good, twice as smart, and work twice as hard as their white peers. Living in this constant state of alert can lead to chronic stress, anxiety, and eventually burnout.

From a brain perspective, this is your amygdala in overdrive, flooding your system with cortisol and keeping you on edge. Over time, it messes with everything from your sleep to digestion, and it takes a toll on your mental and physical health.

Self-Permission: "I give myself permission to stand down. I am safe in this moment. I belong here. I can respond to what's real, not just what I fear."

The way to break free from this saboteur is to move away from survival mode to a mindset that allows for growth, creativity, and connection. For my clients, this means getting real evidence to challenge their hypervigilant thoughts. They write down affirmations and accomplishments that remind them they belong in the spaces they're in and have earned their success (throwback to the Three-by-Three Challenge). This does two things: It pushes back against the saboteur's narrative, and it engages the rational part of the brain—the prefrontal cortex. Over time, this helps to rewire those overactive neural pathways and creates a healthier, more balanced mental state.

By practicing this regularly, they show their brains that constant alertness isn't necessary. They rewrite the narrative and build a self-fulfilling prophecy of confidence and belonging, one that helps them thrive instead of just surviving.

The Scorekeeper or Hyper-Achiever: Ah, the saboteur I know most intimately. The one that ties your self-worth to your latest win or your next achievement. The one that makes you believe your value comes from what you produce, not who you are.

You know how this plays out: Achievement becomes your oxygen. When things go well, you soar, and when they don't, you spiral. Remember that course launch I mentioned earlier, the one that flopped despite all my planning, hiring, and prepping? Of course you do. I've mentioned it about seven times in this book. Why? Because that failure *shattered* me. In that moment, I couldn't separate what I did from who I was.

If this sounds familiar, welcome to the club! Here, the absence of a "gold star" feels like a failure. It's an exhausting mindset that turns your self-esteem into a rollercoaster, with highs and lows determined by external validation. It also paralyzes you with a fear of failure, keeping you from taking risks that could lead to growth and fulfillment.

The way out? Shift your focus from chasing achievements to building habits in line with your core values.

Self-Permission: "I give myself permission to define success by alignment with my values, not by external validation. I am worthy, even when I am not achieving."

Take my client, Althea, for example. Ambitious and hardworking, she seemed to have it all together on the surface, but inside, she was drained. Her long hours at work left her disconnected from her family and with no time for hobbies or joy. When we started working together, she broke down in tears, feeling stuck and questioning her ability to handle anything more.

As we unpacked her burnout, we found the root cause: She had tied her self-worth to her professional achievements. Her internal dialogue told her, *You're only valuable if you're achieving more.* Things like competence and success had become her measuring sticks, and the weight of those expectations had become unbearable.

We worked together to redefine what mattered most to her, uncovering values like unity, knowledge, kindness, and togetherness. The more she leaned into these, the more her perspective shifted. She found that when she let go of the scorekeeping and focused on living in alignment with her values, her work improved naturally, and she felt far more fulfilled.

The lesson here? Achievement can't be the basis of your self-worth. Instead, let it be a natural result of living true to who you are. That's how you break free from the emotional rollercoaster and find lasting peace and success.

Put It into Practice: Your Self-Permission Plan

You've explored how your inner saboteurs might be holding you back. Now it's time to get practical. Use this exercise to identify where you need self-permission and how you'll grant it.

Step 1: Identify your saboteur

Reflect on the patterns described. Which of these do you recognize most in yourself right now?

- ☐ The Perfectionist

- ☐ The Hypervigilant

- ☐ The Scorekeeper/Hyper-Achiever

- ☐ Another (describe):

Reflection:

How does this saboteur most often show up in your day-to-day life or in pursuing your goals?

Step 2: Name the fear beneath it

What's the core fear driving this saboteur? (e.g., fear of failure, rejection, irrelevance, being seen as weak)

Step 3: Grant yourself permission

Write your personal self-permission statement—something that gives you room to move forward despite the saboteur's voice.

Examples: *"I give myself permission to try before I feel ready." "I give myself permission to rest without guilt." "I give myself permission to succeed without needing everyone's approval."*

Your self-permission:

Step 4: A small experiment

What is one small, tangible action you can take this week to practice this self-permission?

Step 5: Reflection on action

Once you've done your small experiment, take a moment to notice:

How did it feel?

What surprised you?

What will you try next?

Bonus: Explore further

If you'd like deeper insight, consider taking Dr. Shirzad Chamine's Positive Intelligence Saboteur Assessment (just search for it online). It's a free tool that can help you name and tackle your saboteurs with greater clarity.

Receipts

You've come a long way from waiting to be chosen. This chapter was your permission slip—not from me, not from anyone else, but from yourself. Here's what you just did:

- **You named your saboteurs—and their scripts**: You identified the voices that have been holding you back: the Perfectionist, the Hypervigilant, the Scorekeeper. You learned to spot their patterns and how those scripts influence your behavior. And with that awareness, you reclaimed your agency.

- You practiced self-permission as a strategy, not a luxury: You shifted from hoping to be allowed, to allowing yourself. You didn't wait for someone else to give you a green light—you gave yourself one. You created space to move, to act, and to experiment without needing it to be perfect.

- You redefined what excellence looks like: You saw the difference between perfectionism and progress. You chose momentum over paralysis. You realized that iteration, feedback, and real-world learning are what create mastery, not obsessive polish behind the scenes.

- You acknowledged the cost of hypervigilance: You understood how living in constant alert mode drains your capacity to lead, create, and show up fully. You gave yourself permission to feel safe, to stand down, and to trust that you belong in the rooms you're entering.

- You challenged your grip on achievement as identity: You saw how tying your worth to your output keeps you on an emotional rollercoaster. You began to separate who you are from what you do—and chose to build success from a place of alignment, not approval.

- You created your Self-Permission Plan: You didn't just reflect. You acted. You named the fear, wrote the permission, and took a small but powerful step forward. You built a repeatable process you can return to any time the saboteurs try to take the mic again.

Bottom line: You've stopped outsourcing your power. You've started leading yourself—with courage, clarity, and momentum.

Your Next Move

This book has guided you through that uncomfortable, necessary work—the hard conversations with yourself that set the stage for something greater. You've learned that clarity is only part of the journey. Without permission, clarity gathers dust. Without permission, the vision remains a wish.

And now, you're ready for what comes next.

Be in the Room isn't just a phrase. It's a declaration.

It means stepping into spaces with the full weight of your worth, your voice, and your vision—without apology or permission from anyone but yourself. It means no longer standing at the door waiting for an invitation. It means claiming your seat, owning your influence, and shaping the room to reflect who you are and what you stand for.

The journey so far—confronting your fears, quieting your saboteurs, granting yourself permission—has prepared you for this moment.

The room may not be waiting. And that's the point.

Because when we don't give ourselves permission to show up—to be messy, imperfect, or bold—we're the ones left holding the weight.

The next chapter explores what that weight looks like: the silence we carry, the resentment that builds, and the power that leaks out of us one unspoken truth at a time.

Success is
respecting myself
when the
conversation
is over

#BeInTheRoom

Chapter Seventeen

Be in the Room – Show Up. Speak Up. Take Up Space.

Because what's the point of doing all this work—breaking old narratives, reclaiming your time, and redefining success—if you're not going to show up when it counts?

Start Here: Self-Permission in the Room

If I had to distill this book into a one-line summary, it's this: Being in the room—the one you've worked so hard to get into—isn't about having all the answers. It's about having the courage to bring your full self inside.

That means giving yourself permission:

- Permission to be messy.

- Permission to be vulnerable.

- Permission to speak, even when your voice shakes.

- Permission to lead, even when it feels uncomfortable.

- Permission to stop waiting for the room to validate you—and start validating yourself.

If you've read the last chapter and still feel allergic to the idea of being messy, you're not alone. High achievers like us—hi, twin—aren't exactly conditioned for imperfection. But it has been crucial for me. This permission has let me take action, try new things, and not beat myself up when things (inevitably) don't work out as planned. Being messy means you predict that things won't go according to plan, and yet you do it anyway because you know the only way to the other side is through.

Your Work Doesn't Speak for Itself; You Do

Once you've started making moves, the work isn't done. The reality is that your work doesn't speak for itself. *You* have to.

A lot of us grew up believing that if we just worked hard enough, kept our heads down, and did a good job, someone would eventually notice. But in reality, people aren't paying attention the way you wish they were. They have their own deadlines, their own pressures.

You are not top of mind. And that's not personal—it's just the truth.

So if you're waiting for recognition, you might be waiting a long time. And if you're hoping someone will save you from the discomfort of self-promotion, they won't.

Advocating for yourself isn't arrogance; it's identity work. It's about saying, *This is who I am. This is what I want. This is the impact I'm here to make.*

If you don't speak up for yourself, someone else will decide your narrative. And their version? It might say you're disengaged. It might say you're not ready. It might say nothing at all.

The Cost of Staying Small

Let me tell you about a client who showed me what it truly means to step into this. Let's call her Nadia.

On paper, Nadia was the poster child for leadership. She ran a large team where psychological safety was ingrained in the very fabric of their interactions. Her people felt seen, supported, and inspired. Innovation thrived; results spoke for themselves. In those rooms—the rooms where she was the leader—Nadia was powerful, confident, and clear.

But in other rooms—rooms with peers or with executives who outranked her—she shrank. Her voice softened; her opinions stayed locked inside. She doubted whether speaking up would be worth the risk. Would her comments be misread as combative? Would her leadership be seen as angry, aggressive, too much? She was, after all, the only woman of color at the table. Staying small felt safer.

And the cost? Those meetings haunted her.

For days, sometimes weeks, she'd replay them in her mind. Every unspoken thought. Every missed chance to advocate for her ideas. She carried resentment, not just toward the people who overlooked her, but toward herself. And it grew heavier with time.

When Nadia came to me, she didn't want another strategy or tool. She wanted to stop feeling invisible. She wanted to stop leaving those rooms with regret. She wanted, in her words, "to be proud of myself."

So we made that her anchor. She wrote it on a sticky note and placed it where she could see it before every meeting: *I want to be proud of myself.*

That became her north star. Not how others responded, not whether her ideas were applauded or dismissed, but whether she showed up in a way that she could feel proud of.

It's been over a year, and that sticky note is still there. And Nadia? She shows up now. Fully and authentically. Not chasing the outcome, but owning the moment. And the ripple effect? It's transformed not just how she's seen, but how she sees herself.

That's what self-advocacy really is: not a pitch, but a practice. One that builds your identity with every "I want," every "here's what I'm hoping for," every "I believe this could be better." It's not about making noise for the sake of it. It's about being visible to yourself first, and then to others.

So when you feel the resistance manifest as a lump in your throat, or the instinct to stay quiet, ask yourself: *Will I be proud of how I showed up?*

Because you don't need to be liked by everyone. But you do need to respect yourself when the conversation is over.

You've done the heavy lifting. You've redefined ambition, questioned your narratives, confronted burnout, and learned to give yourself permission. And now, this is the moment those choices were leading to.

What It Means to Be in the Room

Being in the room means you stop waiting for permission.

It means you stop shrinking to fit the comfort of others.

It means you choose pride in how you show up over perfection in how you're received.

It means you stop tying your worth to what the room thinks of you, and start tying it to how truthfully and powerfully you inhabit your space.

It means you see that the work you've done up to this point—the self-reflection, the boundary setting, the redefinition of success—was all to prepare you for *this*.

Because this is the room where your authentic self belongs.

Your Next Step: Step into the Room

Phew!

I see you. The work you've done to get here, the chapters you've reflected on, the stories you've unpacked, the limiting beliefs you've challenged.

When you opened this book, you might've carried questions like:

- *How do I get unstuck?*

- *What's next for me?*

- *How do I stop shrinking and start leading with intention?*

You might've been holding on to guilt for wanting more, or fear that your voice wouldn't be enough in the rooms that matter most. You might've told yourself stories about staying small, staying safe, or staying quiet, even when every part of you knew you were meant for something more.

And yet here you are.

- You've untangled the stories that kept you in survival mode.

- You've challenged old identities and rewritten your own narrative.

- You've explored your ambition, defined your version of success, and reclaimed your time.

- You've questioned the grind, prioritized your values, and practiced boundaries rooted in care.

- You've stopped waiting for permission, and started giving it to yourself.

This wasn't a book about productivity hacks or leadership tactics. It was a book about power—*yours*. The kind of power that comes from clarity, conviction, and conscious action. The kind that refuses to wait for a seat at the table and instead brings your full self into the room, with intention.

You didn't just read this book. You moved through it. And that means you're not the same person who picked it up.

So what's your next step?

It's not to be perfect. It's not to have all the answers. It's to keep showing up—with courage, with self-trust, with the voice you've fought hard to find.

But let's be clear: this work isn't "done." There's no finish line where everything feels easy and certain from here on out. There will still be moments of doubt, resistance, fear. But you have *proof* that you can meet yourself in the mirror, even on the hardest days, and choose now. You have tools, language, and a blueprint. And most of all, you have *you* to lead anyway.

Because being in the room is, at its core, about **agency**. It's not about who invites you. It's about how you show up when you arrive.

From here, your work is to keep showing up with courage, with clarity, and without apology. You're not waiting for someone to hand you a seat anymore. You're choosing your seat. You're shaping the room.

And you're doing it on your terms.

BE IN THE ROOM

#BeInTheRoom

Afterword
Still Learning to Be in the Room

I wrote a book about being in the room, and still found myself shrinking when it came time to talk about it.

I'll be honest: I almost never wrote this section in fear that I would diminish my credibility.

After all, here I am at the end of these pages, and what I want to tell you is this: I still wrestle with the very things I've encouraged you to overcome.

The truth is, leaving corporate to launch my own business, thousands of hours of coaching and facilitation, and even writing this book didn't fix me—because I wasn't broken. It hasn't silenced my inner critic. It hasn't erased the doubts that creep in when I step into new rooms, new challenges, or new versions of myself. What it has done is remind me over and over that this work is never done. And that's okay. What it did was stretch me. It reminded me that courage is a daily practice.

One of the hardest parts of this journey? Telling people about the book.

Sounds simple. You write a book, you're proud, you share it, right?

But that's not what happened. When a friend casually asked me what was new in my business, I froze and changed the subject. I minimized my excitement, my progress, my work. And afterward, I booked a coaching session with my own coach to sit with the uncomfortable truth of why.

It hit me hard in that session: I could talk about the book on social media, I could polish the message, I could edit the content. But in real life, I was shrinking. I wasn't standing behind my work. I wasn't embodying what it means to be in the room.

Because sharing this book means showing more of myself. It means standing up and saying, *"This is what I believe in. This is what I want to say to the world."* And that is vulnerable in a way that's hard to explain unless you've been there. Suddenly, it's not just about the work—it's about me. My ideas. My face on the cover. My voice in your hands.

And then came the photoshoot. I told myself I should be excited, and in some ways, I was. But underneath that excitement was apprehension. A voice whispering: *Who do you think you are, putting your face on a book cover? Why would anyone want to buy a book with you on it?*

That's the voice I thought I had outgrown. The one I thought I had quieted. But here it was again, loud as ever. And in those moments, I felt small. I felt exposed. And honestly? I felt like maybe I should just stay quiet a little longer.

But here's what I've learned through this process, and what I hope stays with you long after you close this book: Being in the room doesn't mean the fear goes away. It means you show up anyway.

I still shrink sometimes.

I still flinch.

I still second-guess.

And then I remember who I am.

I remember what I've already done.

And I walk through the door anyway.

That's what I did. I showed up for that photoshoot, resistance and all. And behind my eyes wasn't perfection, or certainty, or unshakable confidence. It was purpose and a steady reminder that I'm meant to be here. That I've done enough to be in this room, and that I'll continue to do the work to stay here.

So if you've made it this far, if you've read these pages and found pieces of yourself in these stories, I want you to take this with you: The journey doesn't end. The inner critic will still visit and doubts will still knock. But you are equipped. You've done the work, and you'll keep doing it—not to "arrive" somewhere, but to keep becoming who you're meant to be.

Let this book be your reminder that I'm in it with you. That you're not alone in the messy, imperfect, courageous act of being in the room. And that every time you choose to show up, you're already enough.

I'll see you in the next room.

And the one after that.

And the one after that.

And when you hesitate at the threshold—remember, you're not alone.

I'm still learning too. But we keep showing up.

And that's what it means to lead.

Your Invitation Forward
Welcome to My Coaching Practice

You've done what few have the courage, discipline, and talent to do: You've gotten in the room. You've built a career, a business, a life that many admire from the outside. But as you rise higher, the path doesn't get easier—it gets more complex. The demands on your time, energy, and emotional bandwidth increase. The stakes are higher, and the loneliness, the overthinking, and the invisible weight? It's real.

That's where I come in. My coaching isn't just about helping you do more. It's about helping you be more—more aligned, more authentic, more fulfilled. It's about ensuring you don't just survive the rooms you're in, but that you own them with clarity, confidence, and ease.

Why Coach with Me?

I work with high-achieving professionals—executives, entrepreneurs, and trailblazers—who don't need another cookie-cutter leadership formula. What they need is a space to think deeply, challenge their own narratives, and strategize for growth that feels right, not just looks right on paper.

My coaching is about:

- Helping you define and pursue your version of success—not the one imposed on you by society, your industry, or your own inner critic.

- Moving you from high-output hustle to high-impact leadership.

- Guiding you through the messy middle, where the real transformation happens.

Common Barriers I See in My Clients

If you're hesitating to seek support, you're not alone. High achievers often resist coaching for reasons that make perfect sense given your journey so far:

Fear of vulnerability: You're used to being the one with the answers. Admitting you want help can feel like weakness, but it's a profound strength.

Perfectionism: You want to get it just right. But coaching is about progress, not perfection.

Time scarcity: You're already stretched. But the hour you spend in coaching isn't just another meeting—it's the one that makes all the others easier.

Fear of necessary change: Deep down, you sense that real growth will require real shifts, and that can be intimidating.

Unclear vision of "more": You want more, but you're not sure what that is, and you're afraid to look too closely at the answers.

I know these barriers intimately. Not just as a coach, but as someone who's faced them myself. I once ghosted my own executive coach for two years when I realized our conversations were getting uncomfortably close to the truths I wasn't ready to face. I know what it feels like to sense that stepping into your more might mean leaving behind what's familiar.

What Our Work Together Looks Like

I offer coaching that meets you where you are and challenges you to grow. Together, we'll:

- Break through the limiting beliefs keeping you stuck.

- Build strategies that align with your values and ambitions.

- Navigate complexity—whether that's scaling a business, leading at a higher level, or designing a life that reflects who you really are.

- Make leadership feel lighter so you can move with clarity and confidence, not second-guessing and strain.

This isn't just another task on your to-do list. The time you invest in our sessions becomes the catalyst for smarter decisions, deeper relationships, and more intentional success.

How to Get Started

If this resonates, I invite you to take the next step: Book a Complimentary Private Strategy Intensive with me at www. beintheroomcoaching.com—a space where we can explore where you are, where you want to go, and how we might work together to get you there.

Acknowledgments

Doing something scary takes a village.

And this? This was terrifying.

Writing a book lived on a sticky note in my "someday" column for three years. Every December, I'd stare at it wondering if it needed to roll into January again. And now, here we are.

The first draft of this book took me two weeks to write. I remember thinking, *That can't be right. It's supposed to take longer than this.*

And it did.

It took a two years of testing stories, workshopping ideas, refining turns of phrase, re-writing cover to cover, and figuring out what actually landed. Most importantly, it took sending early versions to the people I trust most for honest feedback, thoughtful suggestions, and the kind of encouragement that reminded me to keep going.

First, to my inner circle and first readers: Christopher, Shan, Mom, Hema, Justin, Stacey, John, Rome, Olivia, and Yancy— thank you. Your insights, edits, and love are all over these pages. Your early words of encouragement helped me to see this book for bigger than what I was prepared to make it.

To my husband, Chris: There were so many moments I secretly wished you'd suggest I go back to a "normal" job, just so I'd have someone to blame if the dream didn't pan out. But you never did. You kept believing. You've always believed—in my potential, my calling, and my capacity, even when I questioned all three. That quiet, unshakable belief has been the bedrock of everything I've built. You are my person. My best friend. My partner in every sense.

To my children: I know these past few years haven't been easy. You've watched your mom chase something big, and sometimes that meant I wasn't as present as I wanted to be. But your notes, your hugs, your patience, your grace—*those* have carried me. I hope this book helps you see what's possible when you dare to believe in something bigger than your fear.

To my sister, Shan: You were the first person to say, "You left yourself out of this book." You were right. Your courage to define success on your own terms has shaped me more than you know. Thank you for holding up a mirror, and for being a model of unapologetic self-trust.

To my parents: Thank you for seeing past who I was and always pointing me toward who I could be. Even when I didn't love the delivery (*you know what I mean*), I've carried your words with me—and they've shaped my values, my resilience, and my voice.

To the brilliant coaches/supporters who shaped me: Warren Baxter, Trina Hamilton, Laurence Anthony, Sue Abuelsamid, Ben Miller, Dave Momper, and Joe Antanasia—thank you for helping me find my way back to myself over and over again.

To Olivia Preya: Your fingerprints are on every page. From your edits to your insight to your unwavering belief in this work, you've helped shape this book in ways I couldn't have done alone. It's been an honor to build this with you, and to watch you build something just as powerful for yourself.

To Keisha Mennefee: From client to founder of Honey Blossom Press to publisher of this very book—what a full-circle moment. Thank you for using your brilliance to bring my words into the world. You said yes to this vision before I was even sure of it myself.

To Yancy: From client, to social media manager, to friend for life—you've believed in me more than I've sometimes believed in myself. And because of that, I've kept going. Thank you for holding me down and lifting me up in equal measure.

And to my readers, my clients, my community:

You are why I do this. Without your stories, your courage, your hunger to shift, I may have gone back to IT, solving complex problems in quiet rooms. But because of you, I get to do work that *moves* me. That matters.

This book is mine, but its heartbeat belongs to all of us.

Thank you for being part of my village. I couldn't have done this without you.